Kingdom RehabHER
Freedom on the Flipside

DANETTE GALVIS

DANETTE GALVIS

Copyright © 2024 Danette Galvis

All rights reserved.

All rights reserved. No portion of this book may be reproduced, stored in a retrieval system, or transmitted in any form or by any means; electronic, mechanical, photocopy, recording, scanning, or other, except for brief quotations in critical reviews or articles, without the prior written permission of the author.

Literary consulting, editing, and formatting by Clara Rose & Company.

Cover photography by Ali Wood, Ali Wood Photography
www.aliwoodphotography.com

Published by RoseDale Publishing
12100 Cobble Stone Drive, Suite 3
Bayonet Point, Florida 34667

ISBN-13: 979-8-9889895-7-8

Dedication

First, I want to thank my Lord and Savior, Jesus Christ. When I think about all the times I've been upset or angry with Him, He was constantly patient! I didn't see the big picture, but He surely did and still does!

Thank you to my husband and children for daily support and love.

Thank you to my family and friends, who have all supported me in both of my journeys of sobriety and real estate investing!

I want to dedicate this book to those mentioned above and to my sobriety community. Some did not make it, and I miss those friends terribly, so this is for them and for those who choose to make a change in their lives and get sober. I am for you!

I love you all and could not be where I am today without you.

DANETTE GALVIS

Acknowledgments

I want to acknowledge and thank all my sisters in the Women's Real Estate Investing Network! Thank you for embracing me as your coach and learning together every week!

Thank you to Tresa Todd, who encouraged me to write this book. Your mentorship, support, and friendship mean the world to me.

Thank you to my tribe of girlfriends. Some are lifelong friendships, and some are newer, you know who you are, and I love you!

Thank you, Ali Wood, for the fun photoshoot capturing the cover photo I envisioned! You're an amazing photographer and friend!

Thank you to those who proofread these pages. Your feedback and edits were invaluable, and your willingness to give your time and support is forever here!

And finally, to Clara Rose, you have been alongside me this entire journey of getting the vision of this book out! Without you, this may not have happened! Thank you for your tips and education on the process of writing to get my testimony out!

Love Always, Danette

DANETTE GALVIS

Table of Contents

Dedication	III
Acknowledgments	1
Table Of Contents	3
Foreword	5
Preface	7
Take Ownership, Choose Life!	11
Turning On The Lights	19
Scope Of Work	27
Get The Dumpster	35
Only One Foundation	43
Alignment Work	49
Major Repairs	55
Change Is In Order	63
Cosmetic Work	71
Punch List	79
Make Ready	85
On The Flipside	93
Resources	101
Remodeling Checklist	103
Train Your Eye	107
Learn The Lingo	113
About The Author	181

DANETTE GALVIS

Foreword

Danette's ability to correlate rehabbing a home for a profit and rehabbing her life from alcohol addiction is mesmerizing, uplifting, and downright profound. If you or someone you know is dealing with alcohol addiction this book is a must. It may be just the tool needed to break the addiction.

The cherry on top is that somewhere in the pages of this book you may also find yourself inspired to learn the secrets to finding financial freedom through flipping properties.

Danette is an extraordinary flipping coach here at the WREIN and her journey to sobriety has been as exciting as watching her rehab ugly homes into something beautiful. It is a joy to observe Danette as she works with our ladies and stirs in them the hope of being free from addictions and financial bondage.

Her legacy will live on forever, not only for her own family but also for multitudes of women who decide to take to heart these words of wisdom. I know you have it in you to be brave and dream big. I am rooting for you.

Tresa Todd

Founder of WREIN, *The Women's Real Estate Investor Network*

Preface

Growing up… there was a lot of church going on! I am the youngest of four, my father left when I was a baby, and I have no memory of my father ever living in the home. My mom took us to a Baptist church on Sunday mornings and a charismatic church on Sunday afternoons. The charismatic church became the foundation of my belief system. There was raising of hands, speaking in tongues, and dancing; it was all I knew. I gave my life to Christ in an upstairs youth service when I was thirteen.

Once I graduated from high school, my way of moving out of my mom's house and getting out from under the strict rules was to get a leasing job. Back then you could get a big discount on rent or even a free apartment when you lived and worked there.

At just eighteen, I got a job leasing apartments and moved twenty minutes away from our Fort Worth home. In my mind, it was just too far to go to church on Sunday, so I quit going.

When I talk about my testimony I often say, "I fled the church because I couldn't be perfect." I did not understand grace, forgiveness, or mercy, and having a relationship with a God I felt like I couldn't please, wasn't something I could process at the ripe age of eighteen.

When I turned twenty-one, I got my real estate license so I could earn commissions for relocation services and referring people to apartments, temporary houses, or corporate housing. I became successful right out of the gate; I didn't even know I was a salesperson until I became the top producer in the company.

A few years into the position I ended up partnering with my broker to open a new location north of Dallas in the suburbs of Plano. I opened, managed, and ran the location for three years, turning it into the number one producing office out of the five locations my broker had.

When telling my story, I often share that, "I lived my life in reverse," since I went straight into work instead of college. I feel like I learned in the school of hard knocks, going straight into work and then owning my own business with my partner. I learned the business, how to run it, how to read financials, learning how to design advertising, and how to manage independent contractors.

Real Estate has been part of my story all my adult life, but that's not what defined me. For years I allowed alcohol and drug addiction to control who I was. The sad truth is the industry lends itself to issues with alcohol. All the wining and dining and happy hours with clients take their toll on many, and I was no exception.

Thankfully, like many addicts, one day, I came to a point where I needed to make a choice. I had hit rock bottom repeatedly until I was finally ready to change. I am forever grateful to Jesus, my husband, and my family, that they never gave up on me.

Even though I have been in real estate my entire adult career, it wasn't until after several years of sobriety, I recognized the similarities between rehabbing a home and getting sober. It's amazing that parallels can be drawn between our bodies and our home.

This is my story of learning to rehab real estate properties and myself! Then eventually becoming the Flipping & Remodeling Coach for the Women's Real Estate Investors Network. It is also my story of sobriety, a story of redemption and hope, one we can all have!

As I weave my story, connecting it with my career, I will give you practical tips on working with properties during rehab. You will soon see how the Lord Jesus Christ created me from the beginning, to be a Kingdom RehabHER!

DANETTE GALVIS

Chapter 1
Take Ownership, Choose Life!

This day I call the heavens and the earth as witnesses against you that I have set before you life and death, blessings, and curses. Now choose life, so that you and your children may live and that you may love the Lord your God, listen to his voice, and hold fast to him. For the Lord is your life, and he will give you many years in the land he swore to give to your fathers, Abraham, Isaac, and Jacob.

Deuteronomy 30:19-20 NIV

You've probably heard the saying; *you can't eat an elephant in one bite*. It's an analogy that means you must take manageable-sized steps when taking on something large, and it is so true. Sometimes a renovation project can FEEL like an elephant and larger than you can manage, especially if the home has been neglected or abused. If you start to focus on the size of the job, you can quickly become overwhelmed and maybe even walk away from a profitable opportunity.

During home rehab, you move forward daily and do what needs to be done that day. It is too daunting to think about everything that needs to be done to complete the renovations, just like being sober for the rest of your life can feel daunting to an addict. But first, you must take ownership before rehab can begin!

Rehabbing a home and getting sober is both a process, day by day, one step at a time. That is why they say don't *future-trip* in addiction recovery! That is to say; do not think about the future and trip out about it.

Even though I have been renovating homes for many years now, I continue to educate myself about the industry and surround myself with more experienced experts. After all, taking on a project and risking losing money is not wise when I could have asked a trusted resource for help. In fact, that is how I became involved with the Women's Real Estate Investors Network, where I now coach new investors. I get to help them, and oftentimes, they help me, that's a win-win if you ask me! You can check the resources section of the book to find out more about the network I'm in!

When I talk about my recovery journey, I must admit it took years for me to acknowledge that I needed help in that area of my life. There were several times I hit bottom and then sobered up for a while, but it never lasted because I was trying to do it on my own.

I had tried to get sober using my willpower, but those

moments of sobriety were short-lived. Sometimes they lasted a month, or three months, and once, I even accumulated a year without having alcohol. All I had accomplished was becoming a dry drunk, a term used for someone who is simply not drinking but not working on themselves. I was not drinking, but I was not happy about it. Eventually, willpower was not enough, and I would start drinking again.

Over the years, the damage I was doing to my physical body was very real, and not just to my internal organs where I didn't see it. Hard falls and injuries were commonplace, so aches and pains were normal. I can't even count the injuries I sustained over the years; it seemed every morning I would wake up with something new.

Later in my drinking career, I was a party of one who loved to fix things. *My bottle of wine and I* would stay up until all hours of the night drinking and working on my projects, climbing ladders, using tools, and whatever was necessary, without any fear of the consequences.

This brings to mind a night when I stayed up late working on a project. We had purchased a home with a 700-gallon fish tank, and we were in the process of turning it into an entertainment center.

I had ordered custom glass shelves so that the lights could shine through the shelving. It was late in the evening when I decided to unwrap the glass shelves and put them in place. Of course, the first shelf didn't fit, even though I had custom-ordered them to fit. I proceeded to hit the glass with my hand in an attempt to force it in.

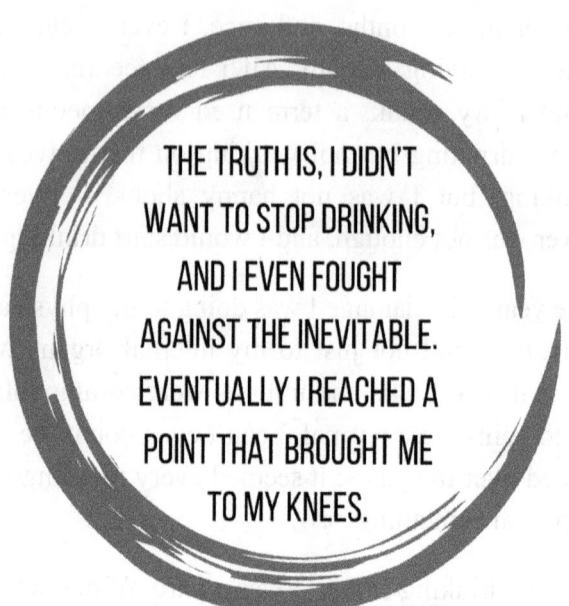

> THE TRUTH IS, I DIDN'T WANT TO STOP DRINKING, AND I EVEN FOUGHT AGAINST THE INEVITABLE. EVENTUALLY I REACHED A POINT THAT BROUGHT ME TO MY KNEES.

I'm a strong girl, so I was hitting it pretty hard, just sure I could make it fit. Well, it didn't, and I moved onto the next shelf. The rest of them fit perfectly.

The next morning my hand was throbbing, and to this day, the bone in my hand aches sometimes. There is even a little bump on my hand, and I am sure I hurt the bone during my banging. It is a miracle I didn't break the glass or fall and break my neck in the process. God faithfully protected me.

The truth is, I did not want to stop drinking, and I even fought against the inevitable, but eventually, I reached a point that brought me to my knees. A place I could no longer refuse to admit I needed help. My breaking point came one weekend on my daughter's birthday trip.

Our family had started the tradition of taking birthday trips every other year instead of having a party yearly. It is a nice change from throwing a party with a ton of presents. We could go to Disney or some location to spend time together and do something special with our daughter, be present with her and build memories.

The year my daughter turned eight, we drove to the Texas Hill Country for her birthday. I cannot remember much about that trip because every chance I got, I would leave the hotel room to hit the bar and my husband would have to come to find me. The weekend was supposed to be about our daughter, but I spent the entire time trying to find a drink.

My husband was so angry with me that as we drove home from the birthday weekend, he gave me ultimatums. I sat quietly on the six-hour drive, communicating with the Lord. I was angry but also fully aware that I needed help. It was time for real change. I had to let it go, I wanted to let it go, and I had to choose life.

I did not want to live that life anymore; I just had no idea how to make it happen. That Elephant was too big! I did not want to die and leave my daughter and husband; I did not want that to be my story. I am not sure if you can relate, but I am sure you do not want that to be your story either! Choose life! I could feel my body dying inside, I was unhealthy, and I knew God was telling me I needed to get help this time.

On the drive home I suddenly knew that to be successful, I needed something higher and bigger than myself. I needed God to be my higher power. He was my only hope, and I had to listen this time.

Inpatient treatment had never seemed like an option before. Who would take care of our daughter since my husband always worked? For some reason, this time, I realized it was different. Now that she was eight years old, he could take her to school and get her home. If he was willing, it was possible.

Back at home, we talked about rehab, and he agreed he could make it work while I was gone, so I began to research treatment facilities. This was something I needed to do on my own. It needed to come from my heart and could not be a forced situation anymore.

It was hard. I had to be interviewed by facilities, telling my story repeatedly so I could find one with an available bed. Talking about my addiction on repeat was not an easy thing, but the people on the other end of the phone do this for a living. They were professional and helpful, letting me know that I was not alone.

There were many tears as I spoke to complete strangers, but the Lord was in those conversations guiding me to the right rehab facility. Letting go of fear, shame, and embarrassment ultimately got me in direct communication with the right facility which was meant for me.

Even though we had good health insurance, rehab was crazy expensive. I jumped on it when I found one with an opening for only $6,000.00. It was close to San Antonio, so it was close enough to home for my family to visit.

I knew it would be hard to leave my family, but they were all extremely supportive, and I also knew the Lord was calling me to do this.

I remember when I went into treatment thinking that I would find these shady people, but NO, that was not the case! Doctors, lawyers, judges, school principals, housewives, stay-at-home moms, artists, and working professionals were there.

There were all kinds of people, alcohol or addiction doesn't care what your profession is. It can consume and ruin anyone's life.

Someone once told me; I was scared straight in rehab; I had no idea what I didn't know about alcoholism. I learned what I was doing to my body, my liver, and how my brain was like a sponge soaking up the alcohol and all the toxins. They were right!

In rehab, I learned to take responsibility for my life, my actions, and who I was. I went from knowing I needed to change to wanting to change. My heart started to change, and I wanted to be sober and take steps to own my side of the street.

Treatment is such an intimate setting; you get to the nitty-gritty, deep, dark pieces of someone's soul. It's hard and scary but so worth it. My roommate and I became fast friends, like sisters. After treatment, we both moved to an outpatient facility, a sober living house for women.

I was under treatment for a total of sixty-five days before going home. Those days and the grace of God changed my life forever. The Lord has been so faithful during this journey; I still rely on Him every day, and I choose life!

DANETTE GALVIS

Chapter 2
Turning on the Lights

"This is the message we heard from Jesus and now declare to you: God is light, and there is no darkness in him at all. So, we are lying if we say we have fellowship with God but go on living in spiritual darkness; we are not practicing the truth. But if we are living in the light, as God is in the light, then we have fellowship with each other, and the blood of Jesus, his Son, cleanses us from all sin."

1 John 1:5-7 NLT

When you purchase real estate for personal use or as an investment, the first thing you do after it has closed and funded is have the power turned on so you can turn on the lights and utilities. You don't know the issues or problems until you can see them. Once the light shines into every corner of the house, you can clearly see the work that needs to be done.

The same is true when we start working on ourselves. Our lives' dark corners and secret places hide the ugly truth and brokenness. Often, we do not even realize what's lurking in the shadows until we start recovery. Our eyes cannot see.

For me, rehab was like someone turning on the lights, and for the first time, I could really see the mess I had made of my life. As I shed light on real problems, I had to let go of shame and embarrassment. The truth is shame and embarrassment were there all along. I just had to finally face them so I could let go.

In recovery, you turn the lights on and shine in your dark areas. Dark areas can be something you have stuffed or hidden away, a memory, a feeling, or even a thought. We do not want to look at those hurtful places, the ones that cause shame and pain.

That's how the enemy wants it; he wants us to remain stuck in our darkness and not find freedom. But there is no doubt or question that shedding light on dysfunction brings freedom. You have to reveal those hard things and let the light in, to be able to move forward and truly stay sober. Just as the word says in the above scripture, He is the light and cleanses us… it's a promise, and His word will accomplish what it says and is set out to do. Free you!

As an investor, I often purchase distressed properties. Someone has neglected the home. The previous owners ignored the dysfunctional places, those broken parts in the home, until they were overwhelmed. They did not invest the time or resources into the upkeep or repairs of the home.

THEY CALL ALCOHOL SPIRITS FOR A REASON, IT'S LIKE SOMETHING ELSE IS CONTROLLING YOU.

It can be similar in our lives when addiction is present, and I had neglected many things: my relationships, my health, and my God.

In anger, confusion, and denial, I fought against God for years. I had not yet learned the true nature of God and did not feel worthy of His love or forgiveness. Once I realized no sin was too great for Him, I could begin to peel back the layers and find personal healing and restoration of my life.

When drinking, there is a lot of back peddling when you wake up in the morning to get back on track. By noon you are starting to feel better, so you have a drink with lunch. The cycle starts again, over, and over, every day. *You grab the hair of the dog that bit you the night before.* That drink makes you feel normal again, but it always leads to the same results at the end of the day, completely drunk or passed out.

They call alcohol *spirits* for a reason, and it's like something else is controlling you. When you are drunk you hurt people. You will do and say things when you are drunk that you would never do or say when sober! Perhaps the reason God says we are to be sober-minded.

You might wake up and not even remember what you said or did. That is where the shame and embarrassment come in. This was true every morning. I often thought I remembered, until someone would tell me how I hurt them.

Before my recovery, most days, I would get up and take my daughter to school, then come home and take a nap. I hid this from my husband because it made me feel lazy. I'd get up around 10:00, but by lunch, I needed a drink to make me feel better. I'd usually have another glass of wine before carpooling. The Lord definitely protected me and my daughter during those days.

I kept mommy wine in my purse, those little bottles of wine that fit in your purse or diaper bag. They are easy to hide. It is a common thing for moms who day drink. Anytime the kids stressed you out, you could pull out your "purse wine." Research is mounting that shows it is an epidemic for stay-at-home moms! Any time of the day, drinking could begin! Play-dates, lunch with the kids, or early dinners during happy hour!

Defeated, I was self-conscious and resentful. I think you can understand why. Shame and embarrassment took over, and I'd often ask God why this was my lot in life. Why couldn't

I just be normal? I was angry at God for giving me such a bad deal. It just didn't seem fair.

I knew I wasn't angry by nature and that being bitter would only make things worse. I had to surrender and own it, so I prayed the Lord would soften my hard heart and give me a new heart. Over time, he has! Praise God, spiritual thinking and prayer changes lives. By God's grace I have been completely sober since October 2015. One day at a time.

At the start of 2023, the founder of my women's investing network encouraged us all to pray for a word for the year. It's a great way to be intentional about what God has for us in the new year. As I did, God laid *WORD* on my heart, as in getting into His word. Be in His word and be careful with my words, which is where it led me! It actually applied in so many areas of my life at that time.

I felt like the Lord wanted me to get into his word and read it from cover to cover. I have been using The Daily Devotional Bible and also following a daily reading plan to complete it in one year.

No, I have not been perfect, but I have been relatively consistent. Even after growing up in church, I am amazed by how much I have learned and grown in my faith from God's Word in a year!

I was reading Ezekiel in my Bible recently, and something jumped off the pages at me: *Dry Bones come alive!* YES, that is how it felt when the Lord started changing me. It was as if He was bringing me back from the dead. He rebuilt my body, and I could breathe again.

"Then he said to me, "Speak a prophetic message to these bones and say, 'Dry bones, listen to the word of the Lord!"

Ezekiel 37:4 NLT

He was telling me exactly what to do… LISTEN to the word of the Lord!" Does that get your attention or what!?!

You may have heard the term *"good bones"* when someone is referring to a house, but what does that mean exactly? It means that the layout and the flow work and the foundational structure are GOOD. So, the house is redeemable without changing the floorplan. So are YOU! The foundational structure that God created in you is GOOD, and He can renew your dry bones.

The bones in a house can "dry out" when someone cannot care for the home like they should. As rehabbers, we restore life to those bones. We might restore the foundation or the roof.

If we restore the wiring, it is like restoring the home's nervous system; if we restore the A/C, it is like restoring the home's respiratory system. Aren't the similarities between our bodies and a home amazing? I will talk more about these similarities in chapter 7!

Another story I recently read in the Word was about a new king who came into power. His predecessor was not a good king, and things had gone terribly wrong. Things had to change. First, the new king had to get rid of all the idols the people had accumulated, and then he restored the temple, which had been neglected.

It says he hired a superintendent, who hired masons and tradesmen to do the work. Evil had crept in, and restoration was needed. Even the holiest of holy houses need rehabbing sometimes! How encouraging is that!?

The wine bottle had become my idol. I would think about it throughout the day and plan when I would be able to have my next glass of wine!

As I was thinking about this first rehabbing step, the image of turning on the lights was so powerful. It might seem insignificant to check off your list but consider the importance for a minute.

The light-filled rooms reveal the depth of the work needed to restore the home. Additionally, you need a light to do the work correctly!

"Jesus spoke to them, saying, "I am the light of the world. Whoever follows me will not walk in darkness but will have the light of life."

John 8:12 ESV

Looking back, I can see the Lord was giving me all the warning signs that things needed to change in my life. I needed to get out of the darkness. I just had to wake up and turn on the lights!

Chapter 3
Scope of Work

"Yet God has made everything beautiful for its own time. He has planted eternity in the human heart, but even so, people cannot see the whole scope of God's work from beginning to end."

Ecclesiastes 3:11 NLT

Now that we have turned on the lights, restoration is possible. We can see what needs to be done, we have to create a plan to make it happen. This is what we call the Scope of Work.

Do not let this process overwhelm you either, it is only an inventory list of work needed. You and your contractor or construction manager will use this Scope of Work when working on the project. It is a communication tool that keeps everyone on the same page. I like to call it the Bible for the project. Your contractor will use this to give you an estimate of what he will charge you, and you both will reference it often during the project for instructions or direction on the project.

The only way to get an accurate estimate of time and costs on a renovation project is to create a written Scope of Work. When you are considering the Scope of Work on a construction project, you have to break it down into each room or area in the house.

When making your list, you can choose to start with the simplest things or the ones that are most logical, like the foyer, which is the first space you encounter. Do the light fixtures and flooring need to be changed? How many light fixtures are there? What type of flooring will you need, and how much will you need? Does it need new trim? Will the walls need to be painted? What color will you paint the walls? How about the color of the trim?

These things are the Scope of Work for that area. Now you know exactly what needs to be done in the foyer and can easily estimate the cost of materials and labor. Simple, right!?!

The bedrooms do not usually need much work. You can paint the walls and trim, add new carpeting, and perhaps install a new ceiling fan. Sometimes you also need new door hardware.

If there is water or other damage, be sure to include those repairs in the Scope of Work. If new closets are going in, you will want to include the design of the new closet. If not, you might want to have the existing closet removed during painting. Be sure to have your painter include the cost of reinstalling shelving afterward, or you might end up doing it yourself!

Easy, right!?! Now do the same thing for every other area or room in the house. Once completed, you have a Scope of Work to be done on the project, and then you can work on how much it will cost you.

It can be easy to overlook items when creating a Scope of Work. Do not make the mistake of trying to keep it all in your head - write it down!

Your contractor will rely on the information on the Scope of Work for each area. If you don't mention the paint, he might think this room doesn't get new paint! Door stops and hardware are easy to forget about, be sure to write them down as well. Include brands, where to buy, and where to place every item. This avoids confusion and mistakes.

It might seem repetitive to write down the same items in every room, like the paint color or new trim, but remember, this document spells out your expectations for each area of the house and will be used daily during the renovation. You can't expect it to be done if you don't include it in writing.

The first time you create a Scope of Work and project cost estimate will be the most difficult. Each time you create a new one, it will get easier. Soon you will know what things should cost and how long to expect the construction to take.

Like learning any new skill, practice makes it easier. In no time, you will be estimating costs and creating a Scope of Work like a pro!

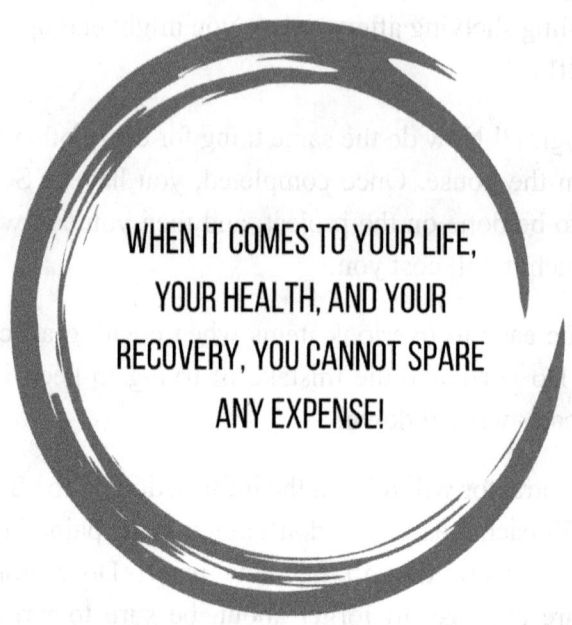

WHEN IT COMES TO YOUR LIFE, YOUR HEALTH, AND YOUR RECOVERY, YOU CANNOT SPARE ANY EXPENSE!

Just like rehabbing a house restores the health of the home, recovery work restores the health of the body, and both require a Scope of Work and an estimate of costs before starting.

Obviously, it will cost you to rehab a house, but it will also cost you to rehab your life. You will have to give some things up, and you might have to walk away from some people.

When it comes to your life, your health, and your recovery, you cannot spare any expense! This becomes non-negotiable if you are serious about recovery.

This is how you know if you are ready to work hard. Do you have connections for private money lending or the finances to rehab a house? Are you ready to pay the costs of recovery and remove unhealthy people and behaviors? Only you can answer these questions.

From a recovery standpoint, the Scope of Work is partially about taking inventory but mostly about being honest about what areas of your life need to be changed or fixed. This is not superficial work; it is deep diving into the parts of you that are broken and not working correctly or serving you well.

This can be difficult when starting recovery. The cycle of go, go, go, drink, drink, drink, then shame, shame, shame is strong. You must pause and really evaluate where you are. You must look at your physical, spiritual, and emotional health.

Once you turn on the lights, it doesn't stop there, then you must create a plan to work on each area!

The Scope of Work or personal inventory becomes the blueprint you follow to create that plan. Just like the contractor uses the Scope of Work to guide your rehab project, you will use your *recovery* Scope of Work on your life's rehab.

So, what is the Scope of Work that needs to be done in your life? What needs to change? What needs to be mended or repaired?

In recovery work, your personal inventory is also where you address issues that need to be cleared up, relationships restored, or you take ownership. Not all relationships have to go back to the way they were, but mending or making amends with those whom you have hurt is necessary. You also may need to process forgiveness of those who hurt you so that those bitter roots can be removed!

I've learned that being offended turns into bitterness, and bitterness turns into anger. That is just where the enemy wants us to be – bitter and angry, which can lead us straight to a relapse! Many get stuck in this vicious cycle, and it's in this work that we can be set free, our bodies restored and healthy again.

From personal experience, I know… you have to change your habits, change your playmates, and change your playground if you are going to be successful. You cannot keep going to bars and expect to stay sober, especially at first.

After years of sobriety, I can attend a party or have dinner at a bar because I changed my habits. Instead of alcohol or wine, I have a club soda and lime to drink; I have something in my hand, and I can still be social AND stay sober.

I also had to change my mindset about things, I had to replace lies with truth. The enemy tells us that people won't think we are fun anymore if we stop drinking. The truth is I am more fun because I love my life and my good friends, and that love is contagious. And now, someone does not have to pick me up off the ground and carry me. I can hold a conversation without slurring my words and have deep conversations I will not forget about the next day.

What does your physical health look like? Do you need to lose weight? When I started recovery, I certainly needed to. It was simply because of all the drinking I did. All the alcohol and the wine, and then, of course, I never felt like working out the next morning! I knew if I exercised, it would purge out the toxins, and I would feel better again, but I had no energy or desire and just couldn't make myself do it. This was another vicious cycle I was in, and my weight kept increasing.

Once I was in recovery, I created a new habit around exercise to regain my health. I found a class I loved and made sure I went three times a week. It was a commitment I made to myself, and it became fun for me as I met new friends who would come to the classes. I was changing my playground.

You cannot stay in recovery if you are still hanging out with toxic friends and listening to their stories about the wild fun they are having. They will drop like flies naturally because they know you are not drinking anymore, and you aren't going to want to meet them at a bar.

When you are in recovery, you can become a mirror to those who choose to stay in addiction; you can't fix or save them; they must reach their last rock bottom and want to change. You have to let them go freely and fight their own struggle. Either way, you must change your playmates.

At first, it was hard to no longer get invitations to the parties, and I lost a lot of friends, but I had to change my mindset about it. Since my recovery, God has given me new friendships that are better for me and connected to me spiritually. I do get invitations to parties and now have a plan if I need to leave; I get to drive myself home, and no one has to worry!

As you consider eating the elephant of recovery, you have to start on the path of least resistance. If physical health is the easiest for you, start there.

In the beginning, it is likely you will not be able to see yourself sober in a year; it is too daunting a task even to consider. Even six months can be overwhelming, not to mention the holidays or special occasions. How can you possibly stay sober during that time!?!

This is why recovery programs break it down into 24 hours or even minutes. It becomes a manageable expectation to not drink or use drugs for the next hour or the day. However small it needs to be in the beginning, that is where you start. One hour becomes one day, which becomes two days, and so on, until you look back in amazement at the years of sobriety.

In 2015, when I finally decided to get sober, I changed the trajectory of my life and the legacy of my entire family. It changed how my daughter is experiencing life, and she doesn't see her mom buzzed or drunk all the time, saying things I wouldn't normally say when sober.

As I changed my habits, playmates, and playgrounds, my mindset changed about many things. I am not the same person I once was. New opportunities have filled my life with new blessings I could not have imagined before, and it all started with designing a Scope of Work for recovery.

Chapter 4
Get the Dumpster

"The priest must order that the stones from those areas be removed. The contaminated material will then be taken outside the town to an area designated as ceremonially unclean. Next the inside walls of the entire house must be scraped thoroughly, and the scrapings dumped in the unclean place outside the town."

Leviticus 14:40-41 NLT

When someone has tried to restore a home, but it is done poorly, we call it putting lipstick on a pig. Doing this never results in a great finished rehab project, sometimes making it look even worse.

We can't just do the cosmetic work to make a project look great, without first doing the restoration work. In fact, restoration work makes the cosmetic work easier. And of course, the restoration work can't start until the demolition is complete. Demolition day means you need to get the dumpster!

The demo decisions were already made during the original walk-through. You decided what would be included in your project's Scope of Work, what could stay and what needed to go!

If you have closed the deal on the house, the lights are on, and the dumpster has been delivered, it is time for the messy work to start.

Demolition work is about getting rid of the rotten and old materials; you must tear down the old stuff to rebuild the new, that applies to rehabbing a home AND recovery work! The goal is to get to a place that is clear and free of debris, in other words, a clean slate. The place where you can do the repairs and begin to rebuild.

You will rip out the cabinets, remove the old toilets, and roll up dirty old carpets that people have lived and walked on for years, and I am sure pets have used them as well.

Some flooring might have old, broken tiles that need to be replaced. They can be tough to remove, but out they go.

Other floors might be hardwood floors that are no longer presentable. You cannot build over rotten wood flooring since it isn't stable enough to hold weight, so if you can't repair it, those hardwood floors go in the dumpster too.

Before you throw out those hardwood planks that are not rotten, consider if you might be able to resell them or repurpose them.

How do the walls look? Do you need to repair some of the sheetrock? If you have any mold issues, you might need to remove more than just the sheetrock. The insulation and sometimes even the studs will also need to come out. All that debris goes into the dumpster!

What does the exterior of the house look like? When bushes or trees get out of control a good trim can make all the difference in the world. This will help make them beautiful in the next season and save you money!

Are there any old structures on the property that need to be removed? If they are not solid, functional, and redeemable, get rid of them. This debris can also go into the dumpster.

On demo day(s), you get to remove all the rot and debris at once! Plus, it's great to see the dumpster truck come and take all the debris away. It is *taken outside of town*, just like the scripture says in Leviticus!

Other things might be hauled away later, like roofing. If you have the roof repaired or replaced, the roofing contractor will do that for you. The roofing demo and debris removal are part of your subcontractor costs, so you don't need to worry about them.

During the demolition phase, you begin to see the property differently. You will get creative because you can finally see more clearly a vision for what is next as you map out the changes that will take place.

In recovery, all the same terminology applies. We must be willing to do the demo work to get rid of the rotten things in our body, mind, and soul. We have to be able to get down to a clean slate so we can have a fresh start as we begin the work of rebuilding our lives.

Interestingly enough, sometimes we behave just like those old, dirty carpets that need to be thrown out. We let people walk on us, mistreat us, abuse us, or manipulate us, and the wear and tear can be seen. Those behaviors need to go, too!

Just like the old shed we tear down on a rehabbing project, some people have to go, and they don't get to be in your life anymore, or at least for a while.

"I am the true vine, and my Father is the gardener. He cuts off every branch in me that bears no fruit, while every branch that does bear fruit, he prunes so that it will be even more fruitful. You are already clean because of the words I have spoken to you. Remain in me, as I also remain in you. No branch can bear fruit by itself; it must remain in the vine. Neither can you bear fruit unless you remain in me."

John 15:1-4 NIV

Pruning is a kind of demolition, but it is a natural part of cultivating healthy plants and a healthy lifestyle! God allows pruning in our lives so we can grow into all He created us to become.

I have discovered my calling now, but I had to walk through the fire and be refined from my addiction. I could not walk out God's plan until I got rid of the junk in my life.

There was a lot of demolition to be done! Sometimes demolition means getting rid of negative thoughts that keep us stuck; mindset is everything in recovery.

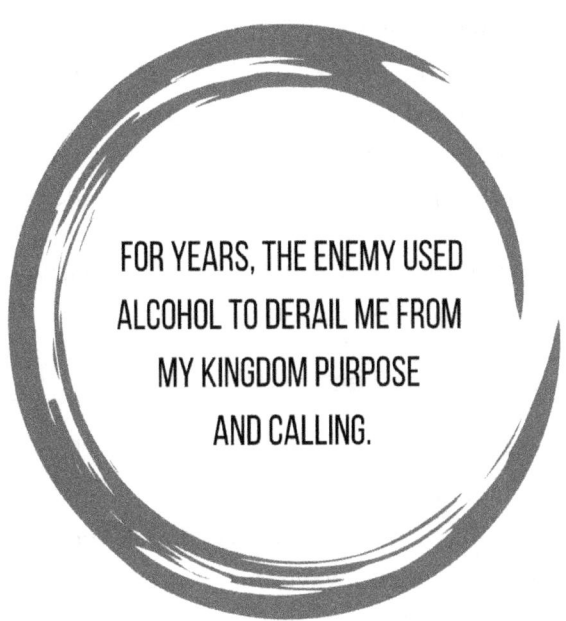

For years, the enemy used alcohol to derail me from my kingdom's purpose and calling. Before recovery, I could never have known that one day I would be looking for a large home to renovate and open as a sober living home. This very week I am looking for that first house!

Recently I had a conversation with my daughter that applies here as well. During the tough times, like recovery or even the teen years, you begin to find out who your loyal friends are. While others are going to parties, driving drunk, and making wrong choices, standing strong in your convictions is important. I keep telling her, "Ask me how I know!"

When we start to make good choices, some of our old friends won't be able to stick around. They will naturally fall away as we start to set boundaries, and we have to let them go.

This is not easy. I remember when I was getting sober, my biggest fear was being left out. You may have heard of FOMO, which stands for Fear of Missing Out! I thought I would not be invited to dinner parties, play dates, or anything that might have alcohol. Fear is a liar. I was not missing out. That is a *seed* that the enemy plants in our minds.

> *"God has not given us a spirit of fear and timidity, but of power, love, and self-discipline."*
>
> 2 Timothy 1:7 NLT

While that did happen some, it had to happen. The work had to be done and I wasn't strong enough to make changes unless those people were at a distance. Over time, those friends naturally faded away, and God replaced them with wonderful people who were healthy for me.

> *"Don't you realize that all of you together are the temple of God and that the Spirit of God lives in you?"*
>
> 1 Corinthians 3:16 NLT

God makes it clear that our body is a temple. When you are stuck in alcohol or drug abuse, you are not serving your temple well.

Before recovery, my temple really suffered, and I treated it poorly.

As a functioning alcoholic, I was always paying attention to when I could have another drink. I realized during recovery that the wine bottle had become my idol. Just like those kings of old I talked about; those idols must go!

Getting rid of those idols, just like the renovation projects, started with debris removal. We must intentionally throw them into the dumpster, and then be willing to watch the dumpster truck haul them away. Gone, permanently.

In recovery they say, blessings will come. It is so true; you begin to see the blessing of making wrongs right, and the blessing of change. I still recall the first time I recognized this truth.

I was having a conversation with my daughter one day. We were sitting on the couch talking, and I was engaged and enjoying our time together. The Lord showed me, in that moment, how present I was. In the past, I would have been distracted by looking at the bar and thinking about when I could have my next glass of wine. What a change and a blessing that came!

At that moment, I realized I had been missing the mark when I was drinking, but on the flipside, nailed it!

DANETTE GALVIS

Chapter 5
Only ONE Foundation

"God was kind and let me become an expert builder. I laid a foundation on which others have built, but we must be careful how we build, because Christ is the only foundation whatever we build on that foundation will be tested by fire on the day of judgment. Then everyone will find out if we have used gold, silver, and precious stones or wood, hay, and straw; we will be rewarded if our building is left standing. But if it is destroyed by the fire, we will lose everything. Yet we ourselves will be saved like someone escaping from flames. All of you surely know that you are God's temple, and that his spirit lives in you. Together you are God's holy temple, and God will destroy anyone who destroys his temple."

1 Corinthians 3:10-16 CEV

I am a believer in Jesus Christ. I am not religious; however, I follow the Word of God and Jesus Christ. My Higher Power is the Highest of them all! In a word, He is my

THE FOUNDATION OF A HOME IS ONE OF THE MOST IMPORTANT PIECES OF THE PROJECT. IF THE FOUNDATION AIN'T RIGHT, NOTHING IS RIGHT!

foundation in life. All that I am and all that I do now rests on Him.

Currently, I am using the Positive Thinking Bible by Norman Vincent Peale for my quiet time with the Lord. I also use other versions, but I am really enjoying this Contemporary English Version and its everyday language.

The other day, I prayed and asked the Lord what He wanted me to say regarding the foundation. He led me to 1 Corinthians 3:10 where I read, Only One Foundation. As soon as I read this, I began to weep. He was speaking directly to me, directly to you!

Isn't that fascinating? Rebuilding and/or remodeling is nothing new under the sun; I love how I can go to His word and read about the exact work I am in! The Lord "speaks" to us through His written word. It applies every day in every way! You don't have to be a believer to rehab a home or your life here on earth, but by God's grace, my faith has brought me out of the darkness and into His marvelous light and will bring me eternal life with my Lord and Savior. He is my firm foundation, and just like a building, I can rest on it.

When beginning any project, you have to make sure the foundation is right before restoration can start. This applies to renovating a building or recovering from addiction!

The foundation of a home is one of the most important pieces of the project. If the foundation isn't right, nothing is going to be right! Things will not line up, windows will not open, and doors will not close properly.

Usually, you can even feel if the foundation is good or not when you walk through a home. A term often used by people in the real estate industry is *the foundation walks flat*! That simply means the foundation seems to be in good condition when you walk through the property; there are no obvious slants, tilts, or other signs of foundational issues.

Of course, you still want to do your due diligence because foundation work can be expensive, and if there are any issues, you will need to budget for it.

Homes are grounded in the earth's surface, weather and water affect how the foundation is connected to the earth. In truth, the house is always settling; it's a natural occurrence. It does not mean there are structural or foundational issues. It just means the house is settling, which is normal. That is not what we are talking about in this chapter.

Foundation issues that are structural in nature need to be fixed. Common signs that a foundation problem might exist are exterior or interior wall cracks, gaps between windows and walls, squeaky, bouncy, or saggy floors, pooling water around the foundation or other drainage issues, nails popping out of the sheetrock, bowed walls, and, of course, sloping floors.

In a home, you do not want to replace windows or doors and repair cracks around the windows, doors, or ceilings... unless the foundation is right. Or else, you will be doing the work repeatedly until the foundation is corrected and things are level.

Often, if you have had to level a concrete slab to get the foundation right, you have to let it settle for a period of time after foundation work has been completed. Remember to put that extra time into your project timeline. Other areas of the project can continue while the house settles, so it is not a complete halt to the project.

If you have had to level the foundation, you must let it settle before you lay tile or flooring.

I would also hold off on repairing any cracks in the walls until the home has settled into the earth for some time, based on the foundation company's suggestions, usually thirty days! Remember, double the work, double the expenses.

Concrete slabs are different than a Pier & Beam foundation, make sure you ask your foundation company for their recommendations.

Of course, no one likes to think about this, but if the foundation and structure is completely bad and unrepairable, you may have to demo the entire house and start from scratch. Hopefully, you discovered this before making the purchase and you have planned for it.

Likewise, sometimes, in recovery work, you have to completely break down all you have known or learned and start over. Before you can rebuild your life, you might have to deconstruct everything that came before.

You may have grown up with alcohol being a part of everyday life, and it could be all you have ever known. Many people in recovery have parents and family members who drink; after all, it is acceptable and legal worldwide.

In recovery, the foundation work that helps us get rid of the old lies, beliefs, habits, and thoughts, is changing our mindset. It is not healthy for our minds to be set in stone. The process requires us to create a new mindset about everything in our lives. It is a renewing of our minds!

"Do not act like the sinful people of the world. Let God change your life. First of all, let Him give you a new mind. Then you will know what God wants you to do. And the things you do will be good and pleasing and perfect."

Romans 12:2 NLV

Now that I have gone through the journey, I can look back at my life and see what was happening during my suffering. He was renewing my mind and preparing me to share my story so that I could have an influence on someone else's life.

I talk a lot about mindset because it is foundational, but lately, the word *remind* has been coming up a lot. The Lord reminds me of who I am, my place in this world, my calling, and of His love for me. Sometimes, we just need a reminder of the truth we have known all along; that our mindset is off, or maybe we have just ignored it.

He reminds me we are all running this race called life.

"You know that many runners enter a race, and only one of them wins the prize. So run to win! Athletes work hard to

win a crown that cannot last, but we do it for a crown that will last forever. I don't run without a goal. And I don't box by beating my fists in the air. I keep my body under control and make it my slave, so I won't lose out after telling the good news to others."

1 Corinthians 9:24 CEV

Years ago, at the beginning of my journey, I did not see how it was all connected. I could not see the big picture because I was angry and still getting through the beginning stages of recovery.

Nearly a decade into sobriety, I can see that this scripture speaks to me in a new way. It talks about running the race of life, but I realize I was injured in my race for many years. I was not racing at all, actually; my addiction sidelined me from the calling of my life.

It is no surprise because that is the enemy's plan. I can now see he was trying to wreck my foundation and take me out of the race. Satan will not come at you through the front door. He will sneak in through the cracks in the foundation. It is time to fix that foundation!

Run your race; keep going. The Lord has a plan for it all and will use it for His good and glory! Today, He wants to *remind* us of His plan for our lives. That is why He planted those dreams and passions into our hearts so they can lead back to the Kingdom for His purpose!

"For I know the plans I have for you," says the Lord. "They are plans for good and not for disaster. To give you a future and a hope."

Jeremiah 29:11 NLT

Chapter 6
Alignment Work

If only you would prepare your heart and lift up your hands to him in prayer! Get rid of your sins and leave all iniquity behind you. Then your face will brighten with innocence. You will be strong and free of fear. You will forget your misery; it will be like water flowing away.

Job 11:13-16 NLT

We discussed the foundation in the previous chapter and its importance in home renovations and recovery. I love how the same principles apply to our lives. A firm, level, solid foundation is essential as a starting point for all of them.

When renovating a home, once the foundation is set, you are ready to begin working on the structure that sits on top of it.

If there were foundation issues, you will likely have alignment issues to address. This might seem minor, but if not addressed early on it can be costly.

You will inspect to ensure that things are aligned and level in each stage of the remodel, but it is most important in the beginning. You must take ownership of this part of the renovation process because you are the one who will pay the price later if there are alignment issues.

There are tools that make this easier; I recommend using a good measuring tape, a torpedo level, and a chalk box. The chalk box makes it easy to snap a straight chalk line between two points on a flat surface, like a wall. It is more practical than using a straightedge for greater distances and will help ensure that things are level.

Learn how to use these tools, even if you have a contractor for the renovation work. The more knowledgeable you are, the better. I often say that knowledge is power when coaching on my calls. You can converse on a different level with your contractors and subcontractors when you have more knowledge.

Do not assume your contractor will be as particular as you are. Go from room to room to inspect the openings and make note of any repairs needed after the foundation is leveled. Take measurements and pull out a level, to make sure things are square.

To ensure things are level, set your level on the windowsills, on top of the window casings, and at the top of the door jams. The bubble should be in the center of the liquid in each acrylic vile. Some levels have a magnetic side that allows you to place it on the side of an appliance for leveling.

Measure window and door openings diagonally. The measurement from the upper left corner to the lower right corner should be the same as that from the upper right corner to the lower left corner. If they are not, the opening is NOT square. Sometimes you can see poor alignment visually, but not always. What you cannot see can hurt you later! For example, you cannot just install a door or window in an opening and assume it will open and close properly. If the opening is not square, it will not function as intended. Windows and doors will stick or not open and close completely.

You may need to add a shim to the door jam or window to create alignment, or if it's really out of alignment, you might even need to reframe the opening. When things are aligned, they work properly.

The same is true for us spiritually. If sin exists in our lives, our alignment with the Lord is off, communication is cut off, and our fellowship with God is broken. Things do not function as God intended for them to, which are for Him to give His children abundant life in Christ, and have an intimate, loving relationship with us.

The enemy wants to sidetrack us from the truth of God's love. Satan seeks to distract us with shiny objects and fleeting pleasures, so we do not stay in alignment with our Lord.

> *Be of sober spirit, be on the alert. Your adversary, the devil, prowls around like a roaring lion, seeking someone to devour. But resist him, firm in your faith, knowing that the same experiences of suffering are being accomplished by your brethren who are in the world. After you have suffered for a little while, the God of all grace, who called you to His eternal glory in Christ, will Himself perfect, confirm, strengthen, and establish you. To Him be dominion forever and ever.*
>
> 1 Peter 5:8-11 NASB

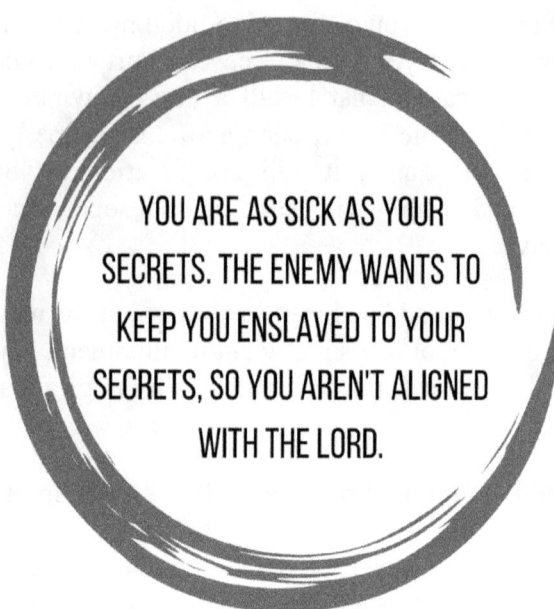

YOU ARE AS SICK AS YOUR SECRETS. THE ENEMY WANTS TO KEEP YOU ENSLAVED TO YOUR SECRETS, SO YOU AREN'T ALIGNED WITH THE LORD.

Alignment is also critical in a renovation when it comes to plumbing. Lines must be straight for new fixtures to be hooked up; if they are even slightly out of alignment, the fixture does not fit properly. You might still have water issues even if you could force it to fit.

The horizontal and vertical angles of the pipes help with the flow of water in the home; without proper alignment, there will be issues with drainage. I love the spiritual correlation in this! The Lord tells us He is the Living Water, and we want the flow of living water to be alive and functioning at its highest in us as well.

Your plumber will use a simple tool called a plumb bob or plummet to check alignment. It is a weight, usually pointed at the tip on the bottom, suspended from a string. Its functionality is based on gravity; when the string is extended, it is perfectly straight and can be used as a reference line, usually called a plumb line. This straight line lets your plumber see if the pipe is *true*.

In addition to proper alignment, sometimes in remodeling work, you have to clean out pipes and even replace plumbing that has cracked or leaked. The plumber either cuts out a section and replaces it, or he might replace all of the plumbing if it's old and rusted. Sometimes, it's easier and more cost effective to cut out the old pipes and replace them with properly aligned ones.

The same can be true of you. Depending on how you were raised, you may need a complete "pipe" replacement in your spiritual walk; a reprogramming of all you have learned about the Lord, and a fresh start, so the Living Water can flow freely through you.

In recovery work, there is a saying, "You are as sick as your secrets." The enemy wants to keep you enslaved to your secrets, so you are not aligned with the Lord. Satan wants to completely drown or swallow up your testimony to keep you from making Christ known. He likes to convince us that we must keep our secrets because if anybody finds out, they will know who we really are. They might judge us, or not love us, so it feels safer to hide our secrets quietly.

Do not believe the lies. The world needs us to open up and share our testimonies!!

"They triumphed over him by the blood of the Lamb and by the word of their testimony;"

Revelation 12:11a NIV

Spiritual realignment starts with confessing sins, which brings freedom. He can clean out those dirty pipes and allow the healing waters to flow in you again. It is essentially cleaning out the lines and realigning for the flow of the Living Water that is Jesus Christ. What a beautiful picture of how the Lord makes us new, inside and out. It will not happen all at once; you must work through stages. You're *squaring up* and day by day things begin to work properly again.

The beauty is that once you begin to confess your faults and open up your heart with honesty, you become FREE. Free to live the life He created you to live!

Once you begin sharing with trusted friends, groups, or a counselor, you become lighter. You feel accepted and loved exactly where you are. Secrets revealed can be healed, and this brings freedom. It becomes an exercise you do not want to stop doing because you start to feel freedom on the flipside!

Chapter 7
Major Repairs

Jesus looked at them and said, "With man, this is impossible, but with God, all things are possible.

Matthew 19:26 NIV

My job as a RehabHER is to restore the health of the home. As I have mentioned before, to do this, it is important to get the major repairs done before you do any cosmetic work, and I shared some of the expensive lessons you might learn if you skip the repair process.

Major repairs are super important for a successful remodel, and you must spare no expense in your budget for these items. It will cost time and money, but everything must be done correctly, and the foundation must be sound.

During demolition, you removed all the old rot, and those

areas now need to be repaired or replaced. Foundation, plumbing, electrical, roofing, HVAC, and window repairs usually come with major expenses, so we call them major repairs. They are the building blocks of a healthy home that functions at full capacity.

The same is true for recovery work. You can't cheat or take shortcuts on your personal rehab and spiritual work because the *halfway-done work* will come back later to bite you! It is essential to get to the root of the problem, which sometimes requires a complete gut job.

Gut Job is a term we use in the remodeling industry. It means stripping the interior down to the studs or structure of the home. This might be done for several reasons.

Extensive damage to the interior walls could be more costly to repair than to totally replace them. Or there might be moisture or mold issues, so replacing the sheetrock and insulation becomes a must.

A common reason for gutting a house is to change the layout. Instead of just removing the sheetrock and insulation, entire walls are removed so modifications can be made to the layout or flow.

Maybe the floor plan was popular when the house was built, but it now needs a new look. For example, the wall that separates the living room and the dining room or kitchen must be removed. Removing the wall will open up the floor plan, making it lighter, brighter, and open for entertainment. Home buyers have recently become more interested in this

layout. Sometimes layout changes are necessary to make a home more desirable.

Just like changing the layout of the house, sometimes in recovery, you have to demolish the old to create a clean slate for the new.

If you were raised in a household with different beliefs that no longer serve you or found that they were not 100% true, you might need to change some of those beliefs to develop a foundation of truth and a sound mind.

Trying to build a new life over old beliefs is like trying to put new paint on old, stained, or dirty walls. The damaged parts will still show through eventually. Prep work is required to clean the stain before you can paint.

Having no memory of my father ever living with us, I often wondered why this was and if it was somehow my fault. I had to learn the truth about it later in life, and it did not have anything to do with me.

My mother worked a lot as a single mom, so my family dynamics were quite different from my best friend's family. My older sister by five years took care of me and was often in charge of dinner for us kids. I can remember her making me take a nap and me arguing with her about it.

My best friend had both parents in the house. The whole family sat down for dinner together every night, and I enjoyed being there and experiencing that. Her mom was always around, and life seemed better at her house.

I am not saying my friend had a perfect life, she might have had her own childhood challenges to overcome, but we did experience life differently. We all do, and we see the world through our own lenses. There might be a lens of abuse, neglect, manipulation, or sometimes even something worse. Thankfully, God can bring restoration and give us a new lens. His lens!

So many comparisons can be drawn between the major repair areas of a home and our lives.

We know now that good bones in a house means the structure is good or the flow of the floorplan is good. It goes without saying, our bones are the structure of our bodies, but let us consider our spiritual structure. Spending time reading the Bible, God's word, will help us develop good bones in our spiritual life. The true way to rebuild our foundation is to build it back on truth. We now understand the importance of a good foundation and that is the starting point for any remodel.

The foundation of a house can be compared to the feet of our bodies. Our feet are the foundation of our bodies. They provide stability and affect our body's alignment, and it's where our nerves end. If our feet are not right, our whole body is affected.

Windows are often referred to as a home's eyes. If you have 100-year-old windows that are painted shut, they need to be replaced. If the seal is broken and the glass has become cloudy, you can no longer see out the windows as they are blurry. You can replace the glass panes, but not the entire window.

Just like going to the eye doctor, so you can get the right prescription to see clearly, new windows give you a clear view. Clear, functional, beautiful windows increase the value of the home and are well worth the hefty price tag.

One could even say the HVAC in the home is much like our respiratory system. If there is an issue with the quality of air in the home, you have to address the HVAC system. It moves air through the house and regulates temperature.

Our breath does the same in our bodies. God created Adam and Eve by breathing life into their nostrils. Breath is life. We need oxygen and fresh air to survive.

The nervous system in our bodies is like the electrical system in a house. Nerve impulses, which tell our body how to function, are electrical signals. They travel throughout our bodies sending electrical impulses that keep us alive. Electricity in the home is just as vital.

If the wiring in the home is bad, things either do not work properly, or they can short-circuit and cause a fire that can destroy a home. The same is true in our bodies. Nerve damage from accidents, diseases, or strokes can destroy our bodies.

Plumbing repairs can be costly but ignoring them is even more expensive! Poor drainage and blocked pipes mean things are not functioning properly.

Our digestive system is much like plumbing in a house, with the often-used expression of having plumbing problems when describing digestive issues.

Take the time to do the work and find out what is blocking the pipes. Research shows that trauma can cause many digestive issues. The good news is that healing from those traumas can fix digestive issues! Our bodies are designed to heal. Our God can heal anything!

In the real estate industry, people often refer to the kitchen as the heart of the home. This is where family and friends gather together and share a meal. It is often the hub of activities and where everyone starts and ends their day, and making a kitchen upgrade is a great use of the remodeling budget. You will most always see a return on the investment if you upgrade the kitchen.

The heart that beats in our chest and *our emotional heart* are just as important as the kitchen is to the home. Did you know if you allow your heart to be open, your mind will follow? When we feel loved, it changes our minds.

When your heart becomes healthy and in a good state, your mindset starts to change automatically. You begin to think differently. You begin to act differently, and you begin to respond differently to situations or conversations. You are not as quick to anger.

If you hold on to anger, hold a grudge, or even have hate in your heart, your whole body reflects it, and disease takes hold. Your face shows it. The expressions on your face as you walk around will show what is in your heart. People holding onto anger usually have increasingly permanent angry expressions on their faces.

A healthy physical and emotional heart will positively impact your entire life. Taking the time to work on heart issues will also yield great rewards in rehabbing your life. You may notice you are smiling more and now greeting others with a smile.

The roof is another major repair that can be costly. It is also vital to the health of the home; it protects everything below it, shelters us from the world, and covers us. A damaged or worn-out roof might leak and cause damage inside the home. Sometimes, a storm might cause roof damage. Whatever the cause, it must be fixed to avoid further damage.

Storms are like trauma in our lives. They often do damage that must be repaired, just as trauma can cause damage to our heart that also needs to be repaired. Let the Lord be the roof over your life and let him heal past damage caused by the enemy, who leaks lies into your life every chance he gets.

Exploring the comparisons between a house and our bodies has been eye-opening for me. It has helped me see houses differently as I manage remodels and prioritize the needs of the home. That is why I continue to say I restore the health of a house so it can provide healthy living for the next family who will make memories there!

Chapter 8
Change is in Order

Therefore, if anyone is in Christ, he is a new creature; the old things passed away; behold, new things have come. Now all these things are from God, who reconciled us to Himself through Christ and gave us the ministry of reconciliation.

2 Corinthians 5:17-18 NSAB

In the process of rehabbing a home, without fail, there are things that need to change after the Scope of Work and pricing are already established in the contract.

When this happens, we use a form called a Change Order. It is simply a communication tool between you and your contractors to alert them that something has changed. It describes what the change is, how much time it will take, and how much it will cost you.

Resist the urge to have your contractor make changes without a detailed, written change order - even if you feel 100% secure in your working relationship with them! This is business; a handshake will not protect you if things go sideways on a Change Order or project.

A number of different circumstances can necessitate a Change Order. For example, a contractor might discover a leak or hidden damage you did not know about, so it was not planned for in the budget. Sometimes when this happens, revising your budget in another area makes sense to make up the cost difference. Changing to less expensive light fixtures, tiles, or appliances can be enough to fix the budget issues.

Some other common reasons for a Change Order are a design modification. This can happen when materials are unavailable, budget changes, inclement weather, damage from weather, or code regulation changes occur. These are unforeseen issues that arise that can affect the design and Scope of Work. It could be as simple as wanting to change a lighting fixture after it has been installed. Maybe it is too small or large for the space. To formalize the change, the contractor would write up a Change Order that addresses the removal of the original fixture along with purchasing and installing the new fixture.

Of course, the goal is to avoid Change Orders as much as possible, since they usually result in project delays and higher costs, but they happen on almost every project. It comes with the territory, so do not let it upset you. Learn to pivot, make the best choices you can, and move forward on the project.

I remember one job that had a strong cat urine smell, so during the Scope of Work phase, I budgeted to remove the old flooring down to the concrete slab and treat it with Kilz Primer to seal it. This was how the contract was written.

During demolition, my subcontractor removed the old, smelly flooring, and then during the repair phase, the painters treated the concrete as planned.

Originally, I was planning to go back in with hardwood floors or luxury vinyl plank, but I changed my mind and decided on wood-like tile because it was more cost-effective. I bought the tile and supplies and had them delivered to the job site.

When it was time, the tile installation crew showed up at the job site to install the tile. Seeing that the floor had been painted with Kilz, they informed me that the tile could not be laid over a painted surface. Since I had already purchased the tile and had it delivered, it made sense to stick with the plan and just have the paint removed.

The subcontractor and I had to negotiate to have the paint scraped off the concrete before they could lay the tile. This added time and labor cost to the job. So, we agreed on a new price and timeline, then wrote up a change order based on our agreement.

It was a good lesson for me and a mistake I will not make again. Even after all these years, this industry teaches me something new on each project. Change is inevitable, and Change Orders are as well.

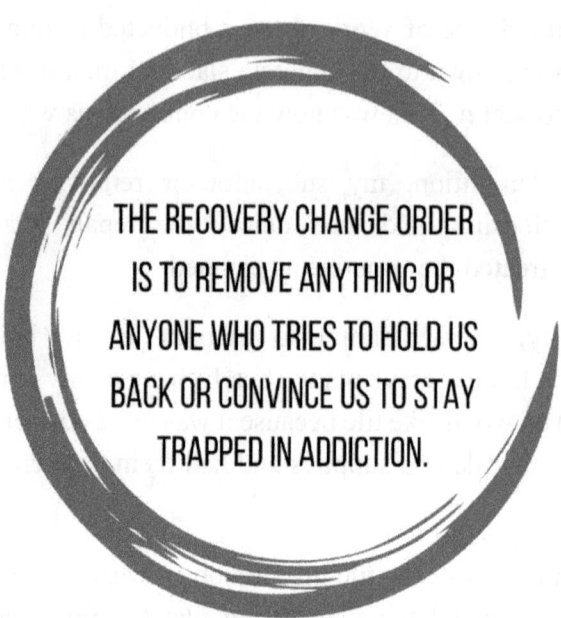

THE RECOVERY CHANGE ORDER IS TO REMOVE ANYTHING OR ANYONE WHO TRIES TO HOLD US BACK OR CONVINCE US TO STAY TRAPPED IN ADDICTION.

In recovery from an addiction, change is also in order. I love the play on words there because if you want to stay sober, CHANGE must occur.

I am talking about changing habits, changing friends, and changing your playground. This change is about making new habits and new friends so that you can make a new life for yourself!

You can no longer play in the same sandbox as before with those same friends. You have to find a new sandbox to play in!

The recovery *Change Order* is to remove anything or anyone who tries to hold us back or convince us to stay trapped in addiction. If you are hanging around other people who continue to drink, the temptation is extremely high. They will harass you to drink, because misery loves company, and sometimes they will win. Therein lies a relapse! Hanging out with those friends is too risky at the beginning of the journey.

If old friends, even lifelong friends, continue to stay in their addictions, we must create a new boundary so we can continue our recovery. We can love them from afar unless they are willing to do the challenging work of change as well. The key is willingness; if they are not willing, you must release them and move forward in recovery.

Friends or family who do not understand addiction can also be people we need to let go of, sometimes only temporarily until we are stronger.

A term used in recovery for those who do not have an addiction is "Normie." They can have two drinks and stop; they have a shut-off switch, and they know they have had enough to drink. We learned that they are normal, but WE are no longer normal, and we no longer have a shut-off switch! They could say, "Oh just one drink won't hurt you."

That is simply not true, and it is a lie from the enemy. We cannot have just one or two drinks like Normies. For us, one drink leads to two, and two leads to eight!

At first, it feels like we are missing out on things. I had to wrap my head around the fact that I was not going to be invited as much as I once was. I realize now that it was temporary and for my own good. I did not need to go to bars, clubs, or house parties. I needed to get healthy and change my playground!

Don't let FOMO keep you from recovery and the life you deserve! Let those old friends, old habits, and old haunts go. Then surround yourselves with those who support your journey in recovery. Remember, fear is a liar. FOMO is not real. We are being protected, and I now realize that we are the net winners!

This can be the hardest part of recovery. You will have to shift your mindset and know you do not need to go; the protection comes from not going. After some time, you could go or stop by, but with an awareness and action plan if you need to leave.

New healthy habits will improve your mental and physical health after all the damage you have done with your addiction. Happy hours now become your workout hour, quiet time with God, attending a recovery group meeting, Bible study, church group, book club, cooking class, or art class. There are so many options of things to do and attend that are different from bars. You just need to be intentional about researching what that may be for you.

Let me get real with you for a minute. Now that I am sober, I love waking up without a hangover. I love not throwing up! I lived that life for too long: waking up to get to work smelling of alcohol, hearing someone say, "I think Danette is still drunk from last night," or getting my daughter to school and trying to keep it together long enough to get back home and get back in bed. That is no life; that is misery.

Just like in construction, as we peel back the layers during demolition, we will likely discover new things that need major repair, and we will need to modify the original plan.

Change is in Order!

There is freedom from addiction, and a new life awaits anyone willing to do the work. No, it is not easy, but YES, I promise it is completely worth it to find freedom on the flipside!

DANETTE GALVIS

Chapter 9
Cosmetic Work

Therefore, if anyone is in Christ, he is a new creation; old things have passed away; behold, all things have become new.

2 Corinthians 5:17 NKJV

Remember the phrase *Lipstick on a Pig?* It refers to any project where someone does cosmetic work without addressing the major repairs first. It might look good on the outside for a little while, but long term it does not last. The dirty pig is still there underneath it all.

Let's take mold for instance. You can't paint over mold, you have to kill it and remove it, and anything that has been affected by the mold has to come out as well. If not, mold will continue to grow underneath the surface. Not just grow but spread to other areas of the home… and fast. It can even take flight to other areas, any place with water or moisture. Mold loves to grow in dark places too. You have to get it all or it comes back with a vengeance.

I think it's just fascinating that the mold situation is even talked about in the Bible. Leviticus 13 talks about the presence of mold on materials, how to get rid of it, and how important it is to get it all. The Lord knows how mold infiltrates, and how dangerous it is to breathe and live with!

Just like mold, any toxic thoughts or toxic upbringing can spread to so many areas of our body and life. All the enemy has to do is implant a lie and wait to see it spread like mold!

A healthy mind leads to a healthy body. Science now understands there is a relationship between our mind and our gut and between our gut and the inflammatory levels in our body. Inflammation can lead to an assortment of health issues.

A toxic mind leads to a toxic body. The toxicity secretly grows in our bodies just like mold in a house, hiding in dark places like a secret. That is why, in recovery, they say, "We are as sick as our secrets."

So many people in addiction try to hide, because they don't want anyone to know they are sick, and there is a lot of shame involved. I was no different.

Often when I was hungover, I would put makeup on to try and cover up or hide how sick I felt or looked. If I had injured myself, I would have to give an excuse to hide the truth.

I remember once, we were rehabbing a house, and unwisely, I was up until the middle of the night working on getting everything perfect, with my wine. I used power tools, caulked, and painted into the wee hours of the morning.

I took a break and stepped out onto the porch to have a smoke. Accidentally dropping my cigarette, I bent over to scoop it up but was so drunk I fell on my face and got a big scratch on my cheek.

The next day I had an event to attend, and makeup was not going to hide that scratch. I had to wear a large hat in hopes of concealing it because it was embarrassing, and I didn't want to explain how it happened or have to lie.

When I was in treatment, they encouraged us to get ready for the day each morning; brush our hair and teeth, take a shower, put on fresh clothes, and maybe even a little mascara & lip gloss. This was to help us grow in confidence and face the day.

When you are working on sobriety, getting up is one thing, getting ready is another, but getting ready for the day can be a game changer. To those who do not have an addiction, this might sound small or silly, but to someone who has been struggling, it is huge.

Before I did the challenging work of recovery, there were major repairs that needed to be done in my life before the cosmetic work could begin. Every day I put my best foot forward, one step at a time!

In remodeling, once you are done with the major repairs, you are ready to move on to the cosmetic portion of the remodel. This means the design aspect of the project. You get to make selections for the lighting, paint colors, countertops, fixtures, faucets, flooring, and more. It is time to dress up the home and be creative.

This girl loves to be creative in my outfits every day, so this particular part of the project is most exciting to me. I love the colors, the patterns, and the prints. But even though I love them all, I must be careful not to overdo it and mix too many different options.

The same is true in the home. Be careful when mixing patterns or colors. It is safe to say one or two could go together, but three or four will make the house busy and overdone, making it difficult to sell. My recommendation is that you stick with mainly neutral colors and only add patterns in a few areas of the house. You want to leave room for the new homeowner to be creative as well and make the house a home.

I also want to suggest that you do not over-improve the home. There is always a budget to stick to when you are an investor. Remember, this is NOT your home, and you will not be living there!

As an investor, your job is to get the home restored and back to health, not to make expensive purchases that price the home out of its neighborhood! Remembering this can help save you time and money!

Now, I am not a fan of comparison, as comparison steals your joy, but people tend to compare themselves to each other. Some people will compare what they are wearing to what another person is wearing, coveting it, and thinking, "I want that outfit." Or they might think negative thoughts about the other person or themselves, "Why are they wearing that?"

That is the work of the enemy. He wants to keep us where we are either sad because of what we do not have... or prideful and arrogant about what we do have.

When it comes to real estate, comparison is a necessity. A comparison, also called a comp, is a comparable property that has already been remolded and upgraded. You begin to look at comps before you make an offer. There is a specific formula that real estate investors use to come up with an offer price and it always involves running comps! If you purchase the property too high and overspend on your remodel budget, you run the risk of not being able to meet the appraisal goal. You will eat that cost difference in the end.

Always make sure the home you restore compares to the surrounding homes that are newer or have been restored. If everyone in the neighborhood has marble countertops, you will need to have them. But if they have Level 1 granite countertops, you do not want to spend the extra money on marble, as you will probably not recoup your investment in them.

You do not have to copy exactly what the neighborhood has done, but stay within the same budget guidelines, so your property has a better chance of selling quickly and for your asking price.

Here is a great example of how you can be creative. If comps used white cabinets in the kitchen, you could use white on the uppers and colored cabinets on the lower. The colored lower cabinets are usually the same price as the white ones, but they give it a more expensive look.

If you see many comps with white countertops, you could do the same but add an accent with a black countertop for the island. I love to be creative, but that doesn't mean it has to be expensive.

This is the ONE area where comparison is a good thing.

In a previous chapter, I mentioned that when I got out of treatment, I found an exercise class I really enjoyed, and I began to go three or four times a week.

This is not a cosmetic action, but it is! I needed to lose weight since the alcohol with its empty calories, and sugar had put excess weight on me.

Getting back in shape, maintaining a healthy weight, and toning are other ways to help build your confidence. Achieving a healthy weight improves your body and your mental state. If you are struggling and want to change a habit, I highly recommend this!

Once you begin to look and feel healthy again, it is time for some cosmetic work, and it may require some shopping. It does not have to be expensive, just fresh new clothes that don't have stains and fit properly. Just like changing the lighting or the flooring in a home, a new pair of jeans and a new shirt can change how you present yourself to the world.

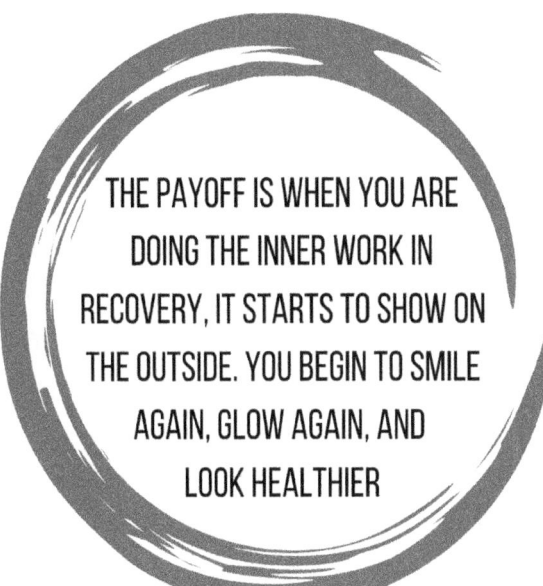

On the flipside of recovery work, the blessings come. The payoff is when you do the inner work in recovery, it starts to show on the outside. You begin to smile again, glow again, and look healthier. You start to look people in the eye and be yourself again. You are no longer faking it and putting lipstick on a pig.

Chapter 10
Punch List

For I will bring you back home again to the land of Israel. "Then it will be as though I had sprinkled clean water on you, for you will be clean—your filthiness will be washed away, your idol worship gone. And I will give you a new heart—I will give you new and right desires—and put a new spirit within you. I will take out your stony hearts of sin and give you new hearts of love. And I will put my Spirit within you so that you will obey my laws and do whatever I command.

Ezekiel 36:24-27 TLB

Now that you are getting near the end of your project, it's time to create the punch list. If you've never heard this term before, it probably sounds a little violent, we aren't going to be physically punching anything!

Although, in recovery, I can honestly say there are times you may feel like punching things. Of course, you cannot punch anything, except perhaps a punching bag in a kickboxing class! That can be therapeutic, and I highly recommend some sort of physical exercise to release some of the inevitable tension.

During your rehab project, once the carpets have been installed, your remodel is almost complete. I say ALMOST because there are always several things to finish or *knock out*. Hence the term *Punch List*.

In remodeling, the Punch List is a process done with the contractor, but before you schedule this with your contractor, make sure all the actual remodeling work is finished, and you are ready for the walk-through. Write down everything you want the contractor to address during the punch list phase. Then, schedule a time for you both to walk the project. This is your opportunity to point out any items that have been left undone or that are not satisfactory. These are items that need to be completed, repaired, or just cleaned up a bit. The rehab project has likely taken several months to complete, and many small things can be forgotten about or unnoticed.

Sometimes, the Punch List will include the installation of items that were delayed for some reason, such as a back-ordered appliance or chandelier. Touch-up painting, replacing trim pieces, or last-minute adjustments to cabinet doors are common items found on the list.

It could be something big or small, no matter the size, you need to include it on the list in detail. If it's not on the list, it won't get addressed.

You will need a roll of painter's tape. Blue is usually my color of choice, but any color that will be obvious and easily seen can work. As you walk the project with your contractor, point out each item on the Punch List and put a small piece of tape on every item that needs attention. The contractor and his crew will complete each task on the punch list and check it off; once completed, they simply take the tape off the item. When the tape is gone, the Punch List is done.

After the contractor and his crew have finished the items on your Punch List and you do a final walk-through with them, the project is now complete, and you can make your final payment to the contractor.

NEVER make the final payment before a completed Punch List and final walkthrough. Sadly, once you pay them, they no longer have an incentive to get the Punch List done. Other work will become their priority, and you might end up doing the punch list work yourself.

In recovery, the inventory list we created is like the punch list of your project. The difference is, of course, that your work on the inventory list starts at the beginning of recovery and continues throughout your recovery process, instead of at the end like a punch list.

You will continue to go through that list and clean up anything still left undone. This might involve cleaning up issues with an individual person, meaning having a conversation to acknowledge something you have done that was upsetting or offensive. It is an acknowledgement on your part and an apology conversation to make amends.

When you started recovery, you created your list, but you should expect it to take time to complete. It can be lengthy, and it will likely grow as you move through recovery. Don't let this discourage you, it is a process, a journey.

Start by trying to have a conversation with the person if they are willing. You must boldly admit your wrongs and ask for forgiveness.

This is not the part that takes long, but sometimes it takes time to set up the conversations.

One of the conversations I needed to have, which was the hardest one I had to do, was with my ex-husband. Thankfully, he had agreed to talk, but I was filled with anxiety about it.

During our conversation, I acknowledged my side of the relationship, and my actions that ended our marriage. I asked for his forgiveness, which he granted, and we ended the conversation with kind words, wishing each other the best in all that life brings. The conversation went better than I expected.

In some cases, the person might not be available for some reason, or they might have passed away. In these cases, you can simply write a letter and ask for forgiveness. This process is obviously about your own healing.

It is the action that brings you freedom, not always the result. It can bring freedom to the other person as well and possibly restore a relationship, but if they are not willing to reconcile, it will still bring you freedom to release the guilt. Some relationships cannot be restored because the other party does not have a desire to restore it. You still need to do your part for yourself. If something was done to you, release and forgive. Do not invite danger or toxicity back into your life.

In my experience of doing this recovery work, I used a notebook to record my inventory list. I wrote out multiple pages on things I could remember at the time. Then I went through my list, trying to connect with people so I could complete that portion of my recovery and move on to the next phase.

As I worked my way through the list and finished tasks, new things would pop into my mind; memories I had forgotten or had not thought about in years. That is to be expected. Recovery is a process, and you might find things that need to be reconciled for the rest of your life.

I promise it will get easier in time. Once you have the first few conversations, they become easier, and you begin to realize the benefits to both parties. That is not to say those relationships must go back to the way they were, sometimes, they will not. That's okay, too. Boundaries need to be set on both sides to move forward.

DANETTE GALVIS

Chapter 11
Make Ready

"A final word: Be strong in the Lord and in his mighty power. Put on all of God's armor so that you will be able to stand firm against all strategies of the devil. For we are not fighting against flesh-and-blood enemies, but against evil rulers and authorities of the unseen world, against mighty powers in this dark world, and against evil spirits in the heavenly places."

Ephesians 6:10-12 NLT

In every area of real estate, you will hear the term *Make Ready*. This refers to the time you will spend getting the home ready for someone to move in, like a renter or a buyer, if you have one, or getting it ready to list with an agent. If you are an agent, then you are just getting it ready to show to potential buyers.

Think of this as if you have guests arriving! If you are having an event, hosting a dinner party, or even if your mother-in-law is coming over, you want to get the house ready for guests to see it.

If you are a first-time remodeler, you might not realize just how much dust comes with construction and remodeling. You will find dust in unimaginable places. This type of cleaning is a deep cleaning that must happen before any furniture, or furnishings are in place.

You will open the cabinet doors and wipe out the dust on the shelves and inside the doors. You will also wipe down the baseboards and trim throughout the house and on both sides of every door. Next, you will clean the windows and windowsills.

Remember to clean the light fixtures that probably collected dust after installation so the light will shine brightly in the new space. Make sure all light bulbs are working properly and replace any that need replacing.

You will vacuum, sweep, mop, and polish everything you can see as you walk through the newly remodeled home. It should feel fresh and new!

Once the home is spotless, it is time to stage it. This is the process of highlighting the home's strengths and downplaying the home's potential weaknesses to appeal to the largest number of prospective buyers.

Staging is essential for selling a home. While it is an expense, it is well worth it every time. Staged homes sell faster and usually for more money.

If you are an investor or are in the industry, you see things differently than a retail buyer. We can see the creative potential in a room without furniture, but a buyer usually cannot. Not only does the furniture make the rooms look bigger, but it also shows the potential buyer what is possible in the home.

Many buyers have no idea how to maximize space using furniture and furnishings. Staging allows you to help them see the potential.

Your buyer might have larger furniture, like a king-sized bed, and the room might not look large enough to fit their bed. Once you put a king-sized bed in the room, suddenly they can see that there is plenty of room and everything will work.

We all know first impressions matter, so don't forget about the exterior of the home. Potential buyers see it instantly when they pull up to the house. If the porch or stoop has room for furniture, add a few chairs to expand the outdoor living space, if not, consider a few potted plants or seasonal flowers with greenery to create a homey feeling.

If your budget doesn't allow a full stage, you can do soft staging. In this method, you create little vignettes of furniture in strategic places and place a few items in the kitchen and main bathrooms.

Even in a full stage for the home, you do not need to stage every room in the house. The kitchen, living room, dining room, and primary bedroom and bathroom are all you need to stage. The secondary bedrooms or the upstairs of the home do not need to be staged.

When you are staging the house, think of it as a marketing tool as well. The staging will be used in professional photos for listing the home and is invaluable in attracting the right buyers.

As an investor, after you have used the photos for listing the home, those photos go on your website and social media to promote the sale of the house.

Then they go to your website as part of your portfolio of work to promote your business for the rest of your career.

Please do not use your cell phone to take photos for this purpose, it will only make the remodel and your business look cheap.

Professional photos can cost you as little as $99 or up to $500 depending on how many they do. Some photographers will take drone shots, so you have aerial photos of the property and the proximity to other things, like a park or other features that might be attractive to buyers.

Professional photographers have the equipment to capture the right angles and lighting, as well as the tools to correct things and create the light and bright look you need. They can also make the grass look greener and the sky bluer or make any other little edits or corrections prior to giving you the photos. Spend the money on professional photos, and I promise you will always get your money back.

Think about it from the buyer's perspective. They will be scrolling through homes on some app like realtor.com or zillow.com, and your photos can make or break a sale. Great photos can capture their attention and make your house stand out from the rest.

If the buyer sees a king-sized bed, for example, it could reassure them their bed would fit. That could be the deciding factor in looking at the home in person. The photos in the listing are designed to get them to the door. If you cannot get them to the door and create traffic, your chances of selling the house are greatly diminished.

In recovery, we also need to *make ourselves ready* by cleaning up and getting dressed for our own self-esteem, to make a good impression on our business associates and customers, and so we can be a light to others who need to become healthy. Remodeling work is always a work in progress.

In our lives, we should always continue to grow closer to God, to love Him with all our heart, mind, soul, and strength, and love other like ourselves. We should continue to change, grow, and heal from our past. Deep cleaning is an ongoing process, and we must continue to get up, get dressed, and face the world.

When I was in treatment, that was something they talked about a lot. Even when it is hard, it's so important to get up, get dressed, brush your teeth, and brush your hair. It is the little things that make the difference, it doesn't take a lot to help you feel more confident each day.

You do not have to "dress to the nines" and get all gussied up to face the world, it can just be clean clothes and some mascara and lip gloss. For a woman, mascara makes you feel good. It opens your eyes and makes you look awake; it makes you feel more feminine. Lip gloss adds a little color to your face and helps you feel more put together.

In recovery, isolation can be extremely dangerous. It is a tool the enemy uses. When we are alone with nothing to distract us, that is where he does his work. Don't give him that opportunity. Every day your goal should be to get yourself ready and go be active. Whatever stage of life you are in, be active in that.

If you are a stay-at-home Mom like I was, volunteer more at your child's school and sign up for opportunities to help out. Showing up and giving yourself something to do is so

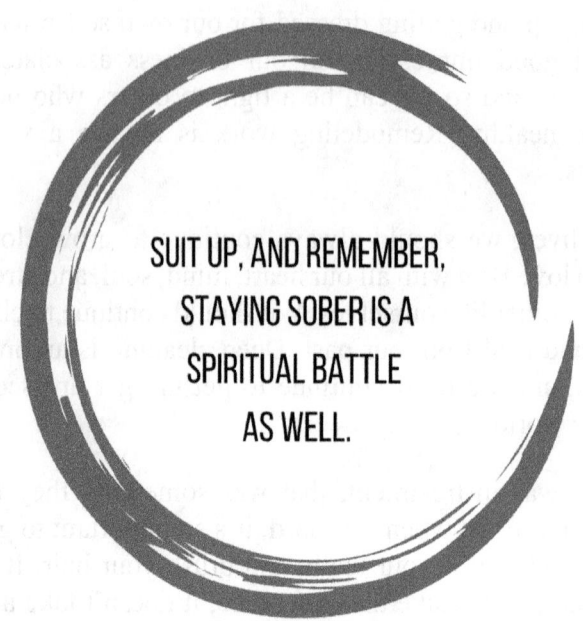

SUIT UP, AND REMEMBER, STAYING SOBER IS A SPIRITUAL BATTLE AS WELL.

important when trying to stay sober, not to mention what it does when your kids get to see you at school helping out!

Some days will be better than others when you start to present yourself to the world. So be kind and offer grace to yourself. It is a step-by-step, hour-by-hour, day-by-day process as you begin to interact with the world again.

At some point in your recovery journey, you may have to start looking for a job, so this definitely applies to getting ready for job interviews. You will be making yourself ready to be hired for a job you might need to support yourself and continue your sobriety journey.

If you are fortunate enough not to need a job for survival, I recommend you look for places where you can volunteer. This will give you a reason to make yourself ready as you put your best foot forward and go help others.

Show up every day at your job or your volunteer work on time and ready to face the day. Before you know it, these will be your new habits, and you will feel more confident and better about yourself and all the hard work you have done to be sober.

Suit up, and remember, staying sober is a spiritual battle as well. The Bible verse I mentioned at the beginning of this chapter is about this, putting on your Armor of God every day. The scripture continues by addressing the different areas that need protection.

Therefore, put on every piece of God's armor so you will be able to resist the enemy in the time of evil. Then, after the battle, you will still be standing firm. Stand your ground, putting on the belt of truth and the body armor of God's righteousness. For shoes, put on the peace that comes from the Good News so that you will be fully prepared. In addition to all of these, hold up the shield of faith to stop the fiery arrows of the devil. Put on salvation as your helmet, and take the sword of the Spirit, which is the word of God. Pray in the Spirit at all times and on every occasion. Stay alert and be persistent in your prayers for all believers everywhere.

Ephesians 6:13-18 NLT

By waking up every day and *making yourself ready* to face the day spiritually, and suiting up in this armor, you will notice the enemy's attacks are more manageable. As awareness of his schemes becomes clear, it will not take much to begin to face the world as your healthy and recovered self!

DANETTE GALVIS

Chapter 12
On the Flipside

You were dead, because you were sinful and were not God's people. But God let Christ make you alive, when he forgave all our sins. God wiped out the charges that were against us for disobeying the Law of Moses. He took them away and nailed them to the cross.

Colossians 2:13-14 CEV

If you read nothing else but this last chapter of the book, and you make the choice to give up alcohol or whatever your addiction is, then my purpose for writing this book is fulfilled.

My mission has been to share my testimony and be an encouragement and light at the end of the tunnel, to anyone who is struggling. If I can help even one person, that is enough. To God be the glory!

Addiction of any kind can be very dark. It might not be alcohol like it was for me. It could be an eating disorder; it could be anxiety or depression.

Whatever it is, there is hope. Just like I have found freedom and forgiveness through Jesus, you can as well.

You might think, "That's fine for you, but you don't know what I've done." Trust me, I have done it all, and the Lord has forgiven and restored me.

Have I mentioned that I have broken every commandment? YES, every one of them! All ten commandments. Need proof? I will name a few.

Commandment 1: *You shall have no other Gods before me.* In treatment, I recognized that the wine bottle itself had become an idol for me. It consumed my thoughts and my time, and in return I consumed it all!

Commandment 2: *You shall not make idols.* See above!

Commandment 3: *You shall not take the name of the Lord your God in vain.* Yep, done that. Any time you use the name of God or Jesus in a way that does not honor or glorify Him, that is taking His name in vain. A surprising number of people do this and don't even consider it swearing.

Commandment 4: *Remember the sabbath day and keep it holy.* Has anyone ever heard of Sunday, Funday? Many Saturday nights turned into continuing the party through Sunday, and they were not holy!

Commandment 5: *Honor your father and mother.* Many times, when I was growing up, I lied to my mom. Even in my adult life, I have lied to cover up what I was doing or had done.

Commandment 6: *You shall not murder.* This is a story I do not often tell, but when faced with a choice, I chose to terminate my pregnancy.

I had been diagnosed with severe dysplasia and needed surgery to avoid cervical cancer. We could not do surgery while pregnant nor treat anything cancerous. If I carried the baby full term, I might risk facing cancer and losing my own life after giving birth. My husband and I were not yet married, so I chose to abort my unborn child.

Immediately after, I mourned. I had been raised in church and I knew what I had done. It dawned on me that I had not trusted God but took my life and the life of our unborn child into my own hands. Looking back, I would have done things differently. Even now I know God works all things for our good and His glory, and I know He has forgiven me. I know our child is with the Lord and we will see each other on the other side of glory.

Commandment 7: *You shall not commit adultery.* My first marriage ended because of my adultery. My guilt was so heavy, I didn't believe it was something we could work through. If I had been sober, I know this would never have happened, or been the result.

Commandment 8: *You shall not steal.* As a teenager, I stole Strawberry Hill wine from grocery stores. Thankfully, things were different back then, and there were no cameras.

Commandment 9: *You shall not bear false witness against your neighbor.* Again, with addiction you are not honest, and integrity goes out the window!

Commandment 10: *You shall not covet.* In my life, there have been many things that others had that I wanted. As a female, we often struggle with wanting that cute outfit or that thing our friend has that we don't have.

There you have it, every single commandment our Lord tells us to keep! Hard to admit, but I am no longer held or bound to that. The Lord has forgiven me as I have acknowledged those mistakes and turned from those ways of living.

If the Lord can forgive and restore ME, why not YOU? He can change your heart and your life if you make the decision to let Him be your Lord. A new life is just a prayer away.

I remember as I was coming out of rehab, my husband and I were struggling, as many couples do when one of them is trying to get sober and there are unresolved issues.

They say, the longer you are in a treatment program, the

greater your chances of staying sober and not relapsing. At 30 days, you have a high probability of relapsing, but at 60 days, you have a better chance of not relapsing, and at 90 days, you have an even greater chance of not relapsing. I was in an in-patient Medical treatment center for 30 days, then I was in an out-patient Sober Living house for another 35 days, for a total of 65 days in treatment.

So, my husband and I were talking about me getting my own apartment temporarily. We were working through the journey of getting sober and we were discussing separation. In fact, one of my therapists recommended not going back home if it was a trigger for me.

I went into rehab in October that year and I was still in treatment as we went into December. I wanted to go home and put up the Christmas tree for my daughter.

One day, I made the three-hour drive home. My husband and I were not doing well, so he was at the office, and I was home alone. As I pulled out all the ornaments from our travels and our life together, I remember thinking, "How am I going to separate all these ornaments?" It might not be important to some, but for me, it came down to that moment.

I realized I was not ready to give up on my marriage and our lives together and I said, "I'm not ready for this yet." It made me dig my heels in deeper and stay, even though it was hard. I remember praying, "Lord please soften my heart." That one prayer changed my life.

I was mad at a lot of things, not just my husband or our relationship. I was mad that I was an alcoholic. Then the Lord dropped the scripture in Ezekiel 36 into my heart, "I will remove from you your heart of stone and give you a heart of flesh."

On the Flipside, I have thought of that prayer many times. He has softened my heart toward everything in my life, not just my marriage. I have a different heart today than I had a decade ago. He removed resentment, bitterness, and anger.

Now, more than a decade later, I can look back and see the big picture I could not see back then. I can see why I had to go through things so I could be right here, right now.

I can help others who struggle because they cannot yet see the big picture. I can be the light to the world that God created me to be.

On the Flipside, the blessings come! I now see this whole journey of addiction in my life has brought me to this day. To author this book, share my testimony, and send it out into the world to do the work God has for it to do… now and into the future. I pray that long after I am gone, He will continue to use the book to change hearts and lives, to help those struggling with addiction, find freedom.

Here on the Flipside, I am in a season of YES.

Last year, I was on a group conference call with a friend, and she encouraged all the ladies to start writing if they had a book in them. She said, "Ask the Lord if He wants you to write a book." So, I did, and this book is the result of that prayer.

There is a line in a song that I love, *with every yes is the kingdom coming.* I get emotional thinking about it. It was scary saying yes and being brave enough to write this book and put my story out to the world. In print, forever, I know God will use it to grow His kingdom.

I invite you to say YES. Say yes to investing in yourself. Even though some may be judgmental about it, saying yes to yourself and going into a recovery facility is not a shameful thing! It is investing in your life and your future. It saved my life!

Say yes to putting on your mascara and lip gloss and showing up for that event or for that coffee date, and stop being flaky. Say yes to creating new friendships and relationships, yes to new opportunities, and say yes to the next project, even though it might be scary.

Above all, say yes to Jesus, follow Him, and He will change your life forever.

All you have to say is, "Jesus, I fall short every day and confess that I have sinned against you. I need you; I believe and trust that you are the Lord. I want to follow you, lead me. I ask for your forgiveness. I want to turn from my ways, show me your ways as I commit my life to you. Thank you, Jesus, in your name, I pray. Amen."

If we confess our sins, He is faithful and just and will forgive us our sins and purify us from all unrighteousness.

1 John 1:9 NIV

Grab a Bible and start reading it! He will begin to do what only He can do to heal you from all the life experiences that have stopped you from your calling!

Resources

For more information on the Women's Real Estate Investing Network and Masterclass, use QR code below.

If you are or want to become a real estate investor, I have included the following resources:

Remodeling Checklist, Train your Eye, and Learn the Lingo to help you on your journey!

Remodeling Checklist

Getting Started

- ☐ Signed contract, executed.
- ☐ Inspection during option period or get estimates from Contractors for project.
- ☐ Complete Scope of Work
- ☐ Complete Rehab budget spreadsheet
- ☐ Secure financing-HML, PML, JV or Equity Partner.
- ☐ Get property insurance quotes, set to begin the day of closing.
- ☐ Provide the lender with a policy number before closing.
- ☐ After financing is approved, set up utilities to start the day of closing. Gas, water, electric
- ☐ Communicate with the Title company on all items needed or requested for closing.
- ☐ Order a dumpster, if needed. Delivered day after closing.
- ☐ Close on property, obtain keys!!! 🏠 🔑

Begin Project

- ☐ Walk project with contractor, confirm Scope of Work and agreements.

- ☐ Demo day! Demo all items being removed from home.
- ☐ Trim landscaping where needed. Remove what will be replaced, demo any exterior items and place in dumpster.
- ☐ Order materials that take time for delivery (appliances, cabinets, windows, etc.), if needed.
- ☐ Repairs first: Foundation may need to settle if slab, Usually 30 days.
- ☐ Make selections: flooring, paint colors, lighting, countertops, plumbing faucets, etc.
- ☐ plumbing rough-in/repairs
- ☐ electrical rough-in/repairs
- ☐ Framing issues repaired or replaced-after foundation has settled.
- ☐ Sheetrock
- ☐ Replace/repair roof.
- ☐ Replace/repair HVAC.
- ☐ Replace/repair windows.
- ☐ Replace/repair doors.
- ☐ Hard surface flooring
- ☐ Tile flooring, tile work.
- ☐ Cabinets
- ☐ Measure for countertops.
- ☐ Trim carpentry
- ☐ Install countertops.
- ☐ Install backsplash.
- ☐ Paint
- ☐ Plumbing and electrical fixtures
- ☐ Install appliances.
- ☐ Install all door/cabinet hardware, bath accessories.
- ☐ Install carpet.
- ☐ Clean

Disclaimer: This is an example for general use purposes, there will be odd items that come up. Every project is different and presents its own challenges! Fix it and move on to the next task!

DANETTE GALVIS

Train Your Eye

This is a helpful resource for learning what to look for when walking properties for the first time, and even what to look for in photos if you cannot get to a property in person!

Often, we have a short amount of time to inspect a property and make an offer. Let's discuss the visual clues you can find to help you identify the bigger issues at a property. First, begin with the exterior. Then, move to the interior for inspection.

EXTERIOR

Foundation: Cracks in masonry. Cracks are common and not all indicate foundation issues. Cracks that widen as they go up do indicate foundation problems. Cracks in tile floor: hairline cracks are common, large, or widening cracks are concerning.

If the crack goes that way, follow it to the wall. Then, see if the wall has bad cracks and if the exterior wall is cracked at that point.

Follow the crack to the wall if it goes that way. Then see if the wall has bad cracks, and if the exterior wall at that point is cracked.

Sheetrock cracks do not automatically mean foundation.

Look for rectangular patches in the concrete driveway or porch. Indication of previous foundation repair.

Ask the homeowner (if it has been repaired) if they have the paperwork and warranty.

Doors that do not open and close correctly and windows that won't open all the way up are also clues that there's has been a lot of movement.

You can put a marble or golf ball on the floor and see if it rolls. Always get a quote

Roof: Curled edges of shingles indicate worn roofing. Dents in the metal roof vents after a hailstorm indicate hail damage and are always replaced. Bumps and lumps in the shingles indicate nail pops. Wind can do damage, and missing shingles are also something that will need repair or replaced if a lot are missing.

Gutters/Fascia/Soffit: Look for damaged gutters that need replacing. Often, gutters can get a coat of paint and be fine. You can also replace only a section of the gutter. Fascia and Soffit often have rot. If so, the rotten sections need to be replaced.

Exterior Painting: You will almost always be painting the exterior unless it has been recently done.

Concrete: Driveways, walkways, patios. Driveways should match the rest of the neighborhood. Cracks in a drive are typically okay to leave if the neighbor's driveways look the same. Power washing concrete makes a dramatic difference. If there are a lot of stains on the patio or porch, try a concrete paint with a texture. There is granite texture paint from HD that costs about $50.00 a gallon, that makes it look amazing.

Garage: Garage door appearance. Sheetrock condition inside the garage.

Siding: Many times, a good power washing is all the siding requires. If parts are dented or missing, if new siding is available, you can patch it in. If it is not, assume you will replace all the siding.

Porches and decks: Look for rotten wood that must be replaced. Sometimes it is repairable or needs stain/paint/sealing. But if the whole porch or deck is rotten, figure in tear-down and rebuild.

Landscape: Is there anything of value that can be kept, or will you have to start from scratch? If trees are touching the roof, they must be trimmed back. Roots can be lifting sidewalks and driveways. If a few bags of mulch will do it, just plan for that. Do not overspend on the landscape. Dark mulch to contrast against the house and a few shrubs or colorful flowers will give it the curb appeal needed.

INTERIOR

HVAC: If they have an A/C (air conditioning) unit but you see one or more window units, assume there is an HVAC problem. The condenser should not be covered in rust. Ice on the condenser or hose can indicate a freon leak, which is a simple repair. Look for a sticker that will indicate the age of the unit. 10-12 years is getting old.

Termites: Dark spots on the sheetrock that brush off indicate termites and tall mud towers near the slab are from termites. Mounds of dirt or wood shavings might indicate carpenter ants.

Insulation: Take a look in the attic to see if there's adequate insulation. Feel walls to see if they have temperature changes along them. That can indicate a lack of insulation in the walls.

Plumbing: Turn on every hose bib, faucet, shower, and tub. Look for discoloration in the water, which can indicate galvanized pipes or water heaters that need replacing.

Check to see if the water gets hot. Look for slow or stopped-up drains. Flush all the toilets.

Look under the sink cabinets for leaks or evidence of water damage. Of course, if the fixtures look bad to the eye, assume replacement costs for those. A vanity or sink cabinet can look perfect to the eye, but inside, rotten all the way through the bottom from unattended leaks.

Also, water heaters should not show any rust or have water around them and should have a sticker with the manufacture date. If it is over 7 years old AND any sign of a problem, you should replace it.

Flooring: Assume all carpets must be replaced unless recently updated. On other floors, see if it looks repairable. If there are a couple of cracks in the tile, maybe there's extra tile at the house, and you can just change them out. Discolored grout is the only problem? You can "paint" grout with an epoxy made specifically for that, and it will look brand new.

Although hardwood floors can be resurfaced and repaired, keeping original hardwood floors is a great cost savings, and buyers usually love that they have been restored!

Tile on walls: Look for cracks and loose tiles. You can replace a cracked tile if you have any to use, but loose tiles often indicate water has gotten behind the tiles in a tub/shower or backsplash. Assume re-tiling will be needed.

Rotten baseboards and sheetrock near a shower indicate a leak in a shower pan. It can't be repaired; it must be replaced.

Appliances: If they look horrible to the eye and are not just in need of a good cleaning (beat up), there is no need to test each one. But if they look like keepers, turn on the oven, and the dishwasher, and test the microwave and the vent, and check the fridge and freezer. If they all work, they might just need a good cleaning.

Cabinets: Kitchen and bathroom cabinetry. Should they be kept and repaired or replaced? A complete gut with new cabinets, counters, and a backsplash?

Windows and Doors: Are windows single pane? Do they have broken glass that can be repaired? Are doors falling apart, have holes in them, etc.? Figure replacement or repair.

Learn the Lingo

A glossary of typical terms used in home remodeling and construction.

A

AC Condenser

The air conditioning unit that sits outside your home. It has a fan that removes heat from the freon gas in the condenser, turning it back into a liquid that can be pumped to the indoor unit.

Addition

New rooms or square footage that are added to a home.

ADU

Accessory dwelling unit. Any additional legal residence that is incorporated into a single-family home. It is also called a mother-in-law's apartment. In most municipalities, an ADU must have its own entrance, its own electrical service, and egress.

Aggregate

Sand, gravel, or crushed rock are mixed into concrete and are an important element in creating a strong foundation.

Allowances

A portion of the construction budget that is set aside for certain items that have not yet been selected. For instance, a building contract might have an allowance for tile if it has not been selected yet. Making all your design choices before construction begins helps a remodel or construction project go faster.

Architect

A licensed designer of buildings. Architects design some homes and remodel projects, but interior designers do most of this work.

Asbestos

A naturally occurring mineral material used extensively for fireproofing and other home and industrial applications. Later, it was found to be a deadly carcinogen. When remodeling an older home, precautions must be taken not to disturb asbestos-containing materials. If this is not possible, they must be abated.

Attic Ventilator

An exterior exhaust fan and vent system that allows fresh outside air to pass through the attic, keeping the home cooler in summer.

B

Backsplash

A waterproof surface (commonly tile) is installed behind a kitchen countertop. It is easily wiped down if food or liquids splatter on it.

Baseboard

The trim board that goes around a room, where the wall meets the floor.

Basement Finishing

The process of insulating and adding finished flooring, drywall, and other amenities to a basement. It is a cost-effective way to add living space to a home without having to add on to the upper stories.

Batt

A piece of insulation—usually fiberglass, rock wool, or cotton—that fits between studs in a wall. Standard widths are 15" or 23". Batts can be 4' or 8' long or come in longer rolls. They are available in various thicknesses to fit walls framed with two-by-four or 2x6 studs.

Beams

These wooden or steel structures run horizontally to support the structure. When a wall is removed, a support beam is put in its place, either recessed in the ceiling or directly beneath it, to support the weight of the home.

Bearing Partition

A partition wall that helps support the structure above. See "Bearing wall."

Bearing Point

In structural engineering, this is a point where heavy loads are concentrated and transferred to the foundation below via a column or other support.

Bearing Wall

An interior wall not only supports its own weight but helps carry the weight of the floors above or the roof, in contrast to a non-bearing wall, which has no structural role and can usually be removed.

Bid

A formal offer from a contractor to do specified work is laid out in a legally binding contract.

Bifold Door

Doors with hinges in the middle are commonly used as closet doors. They can be used in tighter areas where a standard swinging door would not fit.

Blocking

These small wood pieces are attached to the framing members to brace them or to provide a place to nail drywall into.

Blown-In Insulation

Loose fiber insulation that is laid down using a blower system. It is commonly used in attics and walls, where it is difficult or impossible to place insulation batts.

Bottom Plate

The boards that lay on the subfloor, onto which vertical studs are attached to build a wall.

Brace

A diagonal piece of wood that holds up or strengthens a wall structure. Often these are used to hold a partially built wall until it is completed.

Breaker Panel

The electrical box that houses the circuit breakers for a home.

Broom Finish

A rough concrete surface finish is achieved by going over the wet concrete with a stiff broom. Commonly seen on sidewalks, driveways, and stairs.

Building Codes

Ordinances that stipulate how a home must be constructed or remodeled. There are international building codes that are the standard everywhere. Cities and other localities may layer on their own codes.

Building Permit

Official approval is issued by your local government, which authorizes you or your contractor to proceed with a construction project. Applying for a building permit may include a review of your building plans.

Bull Nose

A type of rounded corner treatment on drywall.

Bull-Nose Tile

Tile with a finished edge or edges. The edge is usually rounded to provide a smooth transition from tile to wall.

Bungalow

A small house or cottage, usually one story. If there are upper rooms, they are set into the sloping roof with dormers. Bungalow-style homes usually have large front porches and sometimes verandas.

Bypass Doors

A set of two or more doors that slide parallel with each other on tracks. Usually used for closets.

Bump-Out Addition

This usually refers to a small addition that protrudes from the side of a house. It is usually smaller than a full room addition, but sometimes larger first-floor additions are called bump-outs.

C

Cabinet Refacing

The process of repainting or applying a veneer to existing cabinets. Sometimes new cabinet doors are added. Door hardware is often replaced at the same time. It can be an economical alternative to replacing cabinets.

CAD

Computer aided design. This refers to using software (rather than paper) to design a project. The benefits are speed, accuracy, and the ability to design in three dimensions rather than two.

Cantilever

A section of the house that overhangs the foundation.

Carpeting

A floor covering made of thick woven fabric with a stiff backing. Typically, carpeting extends wall-to-wall. Carpet can be made from various materials, including nylon, olefin, polyester, and natural wool. Carpeting is rated by its density, stain resistance, and wear resistance. It is usually underlaid with a foam carpet pad to make it more comfortable and wear longer.

Casement Window

A window that hinges on the side and opens like a door.

Cathedral Ceiling

A slanted ceiling that rises through more than one floor.

Caulk

A flexible material used to fill gaps, caulk dries hard, but most are designed to stretch. Caulk can be painted, and other types are formulated to be waterproof and resist mold in damp environments.

Carpenter

A person who works with or repairs wood in homes.

Cedar Shakes

A shake is split from a log, sometimes by hand, into a wedge shape. It can be used for roofing or, more commonly, for siding. It differs different from a wood shingle, milled from a solid wood block.

Ceiling Joist

Parallel framing members that span ceiling sections to support ceiling loads. These usually rest on load-bearing walls.

Cement

The adhesive element in concrete. Usually, Portland cement comes in a white powder form.

Ceramic Tile

A clay tile is usually fired and glazed and is used for flooring, shower enclosures, and walls.

Certificate of Occupancy

A document issued by a municipality that certifies that the building is *in compliance* with building codes and has been deemed habitable.

CFM

Cubic feet per minute. It is a unit of measurement for the air volume a blower or exhaust fan can move.

Chair Rail

A piece of trim that is installed 3 or 4 feet above the floor, which keeps chair backs from damaging the wall.

Chalk Line

A straight line created by stretching a piece of string covered in chalk dust between two points and then snapping it down. This is a quick and straightforward way for carpenters to align walls, lay out a space, or mark a series of cuts.

Change Order

When a decision or need to change a construction project or the terms of the contract is made, the parties must sign a written change order to record their approval.

Chase

An enclosed space that is framed into a wall for plumbing or electrical wires to pass through, unobstructed.

Chipboard

Also called oriented-strand board (OSB), this manufactured wood panel is comprised of 1" - 2" wood chips compressed and glued together. It is often used in the place of plywood for exterior sheathing.

Circuit Breaker

Found in the home's electrical panel. Are designed to trip automatically if there is a dangerous short.

Clean Out

An opening through which a drain line can be accessed. Usually closed with a threaded plug, which can be opened and closed as needed.

Cold Air Return

The ducts carry cool room air back to the furnace, where it is reheated.

Column

A vertical support that carries the weight of the building above it. Commonly made of concrete or steel.

Concrete

A mix of sand, gravel, Portland cement, and water. Usually, the material of choice for foundations, slabs, and large, structural columns.

Concrete Block

Sometimes called a cinder block, it is a hollow concrete brick that is usually 8" x 8" x 16" in size and can be reinforced with rebar.

Conduit

A small metal pipe that electrical wiring is run through.

Contract

A legal document between two or more entities. In the case of a remodeling project, you may sign contracts with the designer or architect and the general contractor. If you choose design-build, you only contract with one company that handles both design and construction.

Contractor

A company or individual licensed to perform general or specialty construction work. A general contractor will oversee almost all aspects of a construction job but is not commonly licensed to do specialty work, like plumbing, electrical, or asbestos abatement. The general contractor will then hire specialized subcontractors to complete these tasks.

Control Joint

Lines are cut into a concrete slab to control where cracking occurs.

Copper Pipe

A common material used to plumb the supply side of homes. Other materials used in place of copper are PEX and galvanized steel.

Corbel

The triangle-shaped piece that holds up a shelf or mantel. It can sometimes be decorative.

Corner Bead

An L-shaped piece of metal is placed on the outside corners of drywall where two walls meet. It creates a perfect right-angle corner that can be coated with drywall mud.

Cosmetic Upgrade

A remodeling project in which paint and other surfaces are renewed, but the rooms' layout and the appliances' positioning do not change.

Countertops

The horizontal surfaces installed in kitchens, bathrooms, and sometimes laundry rooms can be made from many different materials, usually ones that are easy to clean and durable.

Craftsman Style

A style of home that originated from the Arts and Crafts Movement. Common features are covered front porches with tapered columns and exposed rafter tails, built-in cabinetry, deep roof eaves, single dormers, handcrafted wood and stonework, a large fireplace, and an open floor plan.

Crawlspace

The crawlspace is the small space below the bottom floor of a home that is enclosed by the foundation wall. Usually, the crawlspace has a dirt floor, but some have been paved with concrete or otherwise sealed and insulated.

Crown Molding

An interior trim piece is used where the angled ceiling meets the vertical wall.

Curb Appeal

Landscaping, the front door, hardscaping, plantings, and other elements that make a home attractive from the outside, looking in from the street.

Curbless Shower

Also called a walk-in shower. A shower that has no curb to step over to enter it. They are an essential element of universal design and a convenient feature for anyone.

D

DADU

Detached accessory dwelling unit. A small home built on the lot of a single-family home. Sometimes built atop or combined with a garage. It is also called a backyard cottage, a carriage house, or a backyard studio.

Daylight Basement

A walk-out basement is a basement with windows and a door on one end. It can be built on a slope.

Dead Light

The section of a window unit that does not open.

Demo

Demolition involves removing existing fixtures, walls, and other structures and materials to prepare a space for renovation.

Design Center

A builder or remodeler's showroom where product samples are displayed.

Design Review

The process by which local authorities check building plans to make sure they comply with building codes. If the design review is approved, a building permit will be issued.

Dimension

The distance between points.

Disconnect

A large switch that disconnects an electrical circuit. Commonly, a disconnect is placed next to air conditioner units.

Doorjamb

The wooden frame is installed into a wall where the door is placed. Doorstops are attached to the side, and top door jambs are used to keep the door from swinging the wrong way and to aid in air sealing. Often, doors come prepackaged with their jambs.

Dormer

Dormers are openings in slopes out of which a small roof section protrudes. They have a vertical wall that can house a window or windows. Dormers can help create more living space in a room with sloped walls. When renovating an attic space, dormers can be added to create a functional room.

Double-Hung Window

Windows in which both the upper and lower sections of glass can slide up and down.

Double Vanity

A vanity in a bathroom with two sinks.

Dovetail Joint

A type of flaring mortise-and-tenon joint that creates a sturdy right-angle connection between two pieces of wood. Dovetails are the quality standard for drawers.

Downspout

A metal pipe carries rainwater down from the roof gutters to ground level.

Draw

Progress billings for projects being built under a fixed-price contract. A contractor will make regular draws from the construction budget as each project stage is completed. Only completed work is paid for.

Drip Cap

A piece of exterior metal flashing or other molding placed above a door or window that keeps rainwater from dripping down over it.

Dry In

When the tar paper or roofing felt is installed on a roof, a home is considered dried in since it is relatively impervious to rainwater at that stage.

Drywall

A gypsum plaster panel wrapped in heavy paper. Drywall panels are used exclusively in homes now, having replaced lathe-and-plaster walls.

Ducting

Light metal tubes carry conditioned air and return unconditioned air through a house. They are an integral part of the HVAC system.

Dust Control

A system put in place by a remodeler to keep dust from accumulating or getting into the air. It may mean dust collection at the source, such as a vacuum attached to a saw or active filtration of the air. Some systems use portable plastic barriers to separate the area under construction from the rest of the home. Systems may include negative pressure, so that created dust doesn't drift into other rooms.

E

Earthquake Strap

Metal strap that attaches a water heater or other fixed appliance to the wall so that it does not tip in case of an earthquake.

Eased Edges

A corner profile for countertops. Eased-edge countertops are slightly rounded on the top-front edge to prevent chipping and make them safer and more comfortable.

Easement

A legal contract allows someone to use a portion of another's property, usually for a specific use, like running a sewer line or a driveway. When purchasing property, it is part of your due diligence to check for any easements.

Eaves

The overhang of the roof past the vertical walls.

Egress Window

A large window can also be used to exit a home in an emergency. Building codes have specific requirements for egress from every part of the home.

Electric Resistance Heater

Baseboard or cove heater that produces heat by passing an electric current through metal wires. It is not as efficient as a heat pump, for instance.

Electrical Rough

A phase of work performed by the electrician. Wires are run and electrical boxes are installed, but the finish plates are not. Electrical rough typically occurs after the plumbing rough.

Electrical Service

A term used to describe the connection from the main electrical utility to the first point of contact in a home, usually the main breaker box.

Electrical Trim

The electrician's final step is to prepare a home for electrical inspection. Switches, plugs, covers, bath fans, and other items are installed.

Electrician

A person who installs and fixes electrical equipment. In most places, a licensed electrician must go through an apprenticeship program.

Enamel Paint

This term usually applies to solvent-based paints that air dry to a hard, glossy surface. There are, however, numerous "latex enamel" paints that are actually water-based but have certain additives to mimic the properties of traditional enamels. Solvent-based paints are rarely used in home remodeling and construction projects now because other safer products have been developed.

Energy Code

A subset of building codes specifically refers to insulation, windows, doors, lighting, and HVAC equipment efficiency requirements. The goal of energy codes is to build buildings that have lower energy requirements.

Estimate

The labor and building materials costs that a contractor speculates a project will require. Often, a written estimate does not necessarily determine the final cost. On the other hand, a fixed-price contract sets the estimated cost as the actual price the homeowner pays for the decided-upon work.

Existing Conditions

On remodeling building plans, the home's original layout is labeled "existing conditions" to distinguish it from the proposed renovations.

Expansion Joint

A piece of fibrous material that is placed in gaps in and around concrete slab sections and the foundation to allow it to expand and contract with the seasons and not crack.

F

Face-Frame Cabinets

A style of cabinetry. If you picture cabinets as a series of wooden boxes, all grouped together. Looking at them head-on; each box has four sides. Following the practices of traditional joinery, cabinetmakers attached a narrow frame of wood to the front of those four edges of the box. This creates a stronger cabinet, hides the edge of the cabinet box, and provides a place for the door hinges to attach to, unlike Euro-style cabinets, which don't have a front frame.

FAR

Floor area ratio: The ratio of a home's total floor area to the size of the lot. Someone in Seattle with a 5,000+ square-foot lot would only be allowed to cover 35% of that lot with a home and any accessory buildings, like a garage or DADU.

Fascia

The boards that are attached to the ends of your rafters at the eaves. Gutters are often attached to the fascia boards.

Felt

A type of building paper, also called tar paper. Usually laid under the shingles in a roofing assembly.

Fiberglass Windows

Windows made of fiberglass are considered to be very durable and are often among the most energy efficient. Unlike vinyl windows, fiberglass windows can be easily repainted. Unlike wood windows, fiberglass does not rot, warp, or degrade.

Field Measurements

Measurements were taken on the home itself. This is in contrast to dimensions gathered from blueprints. An important first step in designing a remodel is to take field measurements of the existing spaces.

Finish Carpentry

The finishing touches after the main structural changes are complete. Includes installing trim, doors, cabinets, stairs, and flooring.

Fire Block

Horizontal blocks of wood nailed between the studs to prevent fire from traveling up through the walls.

Fixed-Price Contract

A construction contract that names a specific dollar amount that the project will cost. This is in contrast to a time-and-materials contract, in which the final cost is not known when the contract is signed. The risk of cost overruns is placed on the contractor.

Flagstone

Flat pieces of stone are used for walkways and drives and sometimes as a veneer on walls.

Flashing

Sheet metal bent into shape to protect the roof and walls from water seepage.

Flat Paint

Paint without any sheen is usually used in living areas and bedrooms but is not commonly used in kitchens and bathrooms because it is more difficult to clean. Most paints used in homes are not flat but have some level of sheen.

Flatwork

A name for horizontal poured concrete surfaces, like driveways, sidewalks, and floors.

Float Finish

A float is a tool used to smooth and flatten poured concrete. It is used after the surface has already been leveled using a screed (a long wooden plank drawn over the surface). Concrete that has been floated will be smoother and more compact and will have most surface imperfections removed.

Floating Floor

A type of floor where the material is not nailed or glued down. Often, laminate click-together floors are designed to float in place.

Floating Wall

A special wall built on a concrete floor has two bottom plates that can move independently. The "float" space between the two bottom plates allows the wall to stay true even as the concrete floor beneath moves up or down. Usually found in basements and garages.

Foyer

An entry hall or area in a home or other building.

Framing

Lumber which is used to construct the skeleton of the building, such as joists, studs, and rafters.

French Drain

Sometimes it is called a perimeter drain. It is a perforated drainpipe in a trench that is covered with gravel. Usually these go around the outside perimeter of a building to keep the basement dry.

Full Review

Larger construction projects trigger a full design review. City officials carefully review proposed building plans to ensure that they meet all zoning, safety, and building codes.

Furr Down

An enclosed area between the top of a kitchen cabinet and the ceiling. It could also be in a bathroom above the vanity for lighting or anywhere in the home to house HVAV ductwork.

Furring Strips

Small strips of softwood are used to shim and level out a wall or ceiling sub-surface.

G

Gable

The triangular-shaped part of a wall encloses a pitched roof end.

General Contractor

An individual or a company that supervises construction. The role is that of a project manager. In some cases, the GC will also have a direct role in construction, but in many cases, the GC will hire subcontractors and tradespeople (like plumbers and electricians) to do most of the physical work.

GFI

Ground fault interrupters are a type of outlet that instantly cuts power if it detects a short. They are required in kitchens, bathrooms, basements, and other potentially wet environments.

Glazing

Installing glass. This term may also refer to the windows in a finished home or a design.

Gloss Paint

Paint that has a high sheen. It is not commonly used on walls in homes but is more likely found on furniture or other high-touch surfaces.

Glulam

Glued laminated beam. These structural beams are made of thinner pieces of wood glued together under pressure. Stronger than a solid wood beam.

Grade

The process of leveling dirt can also mean the level of the ground at a certain point. For instance, most basements are "below grade."

Granite

A type of igneous rock. Commonly used as a countertop material in homes.

Greywater

Wastewater from sinks, tubs, and washing machines. It is sometimes recycled for use in irrigation.

Green Building

A building that is designed to reduce harmful impacts on the environment through its design, materials, and reduced ongoing energy needs.

Greenboard

It is a type of drywall with some water-resistant properties and is commonly used for walls in damp areas. It is no longer used as a direct backer for tile in shower surrounds because it was found not to be water resistant enough. AKA Hardi-backer.

Grout

A special type of decorative mortar that fills the space between tiles.

Gutter

A metal or vinyl conduit that carries rainwater from the roof to downspouts. Typically attached to the fascia board.

H

Handyman

Someone who specializes in small home repairs and improvements. Usually a sole proprietor. A handyperson may or may not be a licensed general contractor.

Hardscaping

Landscaping elements are made of stone, concrete, tile, or brick, such as paths, walkways, and driveways, as opposed to plantings.

Hardwood

Wood from broad-leafed trees, such as oak, ash, and maple. As opposed to softwood, which comes from coniferous trees.

Header

A beam that spans the opening for a window, door, or stairway.

Heat Pump

A device that transfers heat from the outdoors into your home. Think of it as an air conditioner working in reverse. Heat pumps can cool and heat the indoor air. They are much more efficient than standard resistance-electric heat.

Heating Load

The amount of heat energy that needs to be added to a space to maintain the temperature is used in calculating the size of the furnace needed to heat a home.

Hip Roof

A roof with four inclined sides instead of just two on a gabled roof. All four sides of the hip roof slope down from the peak. It does not have a gable or a flat end.

Hose Bib

A plumbing fitting to which a hose can be attached. It usually has a valve and is commonly placed around the outside perimeter of a home so that irrigation hoses can be connected.

House Lifting

The process of jacking up a house to rebuild the foundation or add extra space below.

HVAC

Abbreviation for heat, ventilation, and air conditioning.

I

I-Beam

A strong steel beam that looks like an "I" on its cross-section. These typically are used to carry the weight of the roof and upper floors across long spans, such as in a basement or a large, open room.

Infiltration

Air that slips into and out of a home through cracks and crevices, causing drafts and wasting energy. The main goal of a home energy retrofit is usually to reduce infiltration.

Induction Stove

Induction stoves are a type of electric stove that uses magnetic fields to heat the pan itself rather than the stove top. They are an efficient way to cook, and home chefs like them because it mimics the quick heating and cool-down of a gas stove without harmful fumes. Induction stoves have a flat glass surface and are usually easier to clean.

Inspections

The local government employs Building Inspectors to come out to job sites to ensure the building is being built to code. Specialty inspectors, such as electrical and plumbing inspectors, may also be involved in the inspection process. Inspectors will check the forms of the footers and foundation before concrete is poured, and they will check the construction methods, plumbing, and electrical before the walls are "closed in" or covered over in drywall. Usually, the price you pay for building permits includes the necessary inspections.

Insulation

Material that resists heat transmission that is placed in the walls, the attic, the ceiling, beneath the slab, around the foundation, or anywhere else in a home. Common insulation materials include fiberglass, mineral wool, cellulose, rigid foam panels, and spray-on foam.

Interior Decorator

A person's job is to choose furnishings, finishes, and other elements that lend the interior of a home or other building a certain look.

Interior Designer

Interior designers are professionals who specialize in the art and science of planning spaces (both inside and out) that address the safety and well-being of occupants. Designers identify, research, plan, and implement creative solutions that make spaces function and look better.

Irrigation System

A system that delivers water for plants, such as a sprinkler system for your lawn. It can be set up to operate automatically.

J

Jack Post

It is a metal replacement for an old supporting post. Most have pins to make their height adjustable. Typically used in basements to prop up sagging first floors.

Jack-and-Jill Bathroom

A bathroom with entrance doors on each end from two different rooms is commonly used between kids' bedrooms.

Jamb

The wood pieces that surround a door or window, including studs and trim pieces.

Jib Door

A door that is designed to blend into the wall or wainscoting. It creates a hidden room effect.

Jobsite

An area of work in a construction project.

Joist

Parallel planks of lumber that support a floor or ceiling. These usually rest on bearing walls, girders, or other larger beams.

Joist Hanger

A U-shaped piece of metal that is nailed into a beam. It supports the ends of floor joists.

K

Kilowatt Hour

The most common volumetric unit of measurement for electricity. Equivalent to 1,000 watts of electricity used for an hour. This is what household electrical meters count.

Knob-and-Tube Wiring

An outdated way to wire a house which uses uninsulated wire supported by knobs and enclosed in tubes where it passes through beams or walls. Popular in the United States from about 1880 to 1940.

L

Laminate Flooring

An engineered flooring product consisting of multiple layers of synthetic materials fused together. It is often made to look like hardwood flooring with a photographic layer applied to the top. Usually installed as a floating floor. It can be durable but is usually susceptible to water damage.

Landing

A small platform between flights of stairs. Usually where stairs change direction.

Landscaping

The process of beautifying a yard with plantings, ornamental features, and regrading.

Laundry Room

A room that houses a washing machine, dryer, and folding area.

Lead Paint

A now-outlawed formulation of paint that contained the toxic heavy metal lead. When remodeling a home, remodelers must test for lead paint and carefully contain it or remove it.

Leach Field

A leach field is a large area of land into which filtered sewage is gradually discharged so that it can leach into the soil. It is part of a septic system and used in rural areas.

Lineal Foot

A way to measure lumber. Each lineal foot is equal to 1" thick by 12" wide and 12" long. So, a 2" x 12" x 16' board would be 32 lineal feet. It could be used to measure cabinets and carpets as well.

Load-Bearing Wall

Some exterior and interior walls are engineered to support the weight of the roof and floors above. They are usually identified by a double top plate.

LOI

Letter of intent. In design and construction, a letter of intent is a document that states the intent of two parties (the builder/designer and the homeowner) to work together. Later in the process, it is replaced by a more formal contract laying out the specific price or other terms.

Lot

A plot of land on which a home is situated.

Louver

A cover for an exterior vent in a home that has diagonal slats that keep out water while allowing air to flow.

Lumens

A unit of measurement for light output. For instance, a 100-watt incandescent light bulb produces about 1,600 lumens. An LED bulb can produce the same number of lumens but uses only about 15 watts of electricity.

LVT

Luxury vinyl tile. A flooring material that comes in tiles that can be glued down or floated. Surfaces are usually printed to look like wood or stone with a photo-realistic, textured image. LVT is considered exceptionally durable and is resistant to moisture and temperature changes.

M

Main Water Shutoff

A valve that turns off the main water supply to the house so plumbing work can be done is most commonly found in basements, on the exterior of the house, or underground for city access.

Mantel

The shelf above a fireplace. Usually decorative in its design.

Marble

A natural stone with a porous surface, commonly used for countertops and tile.

Marmoleum

Forbo-Nairn's brand is named linoleum flooring. Marmoleum is LEED-certified because it is hypoallergenic and made with all-natural products.

Masonry

Brick, stone, and other building materials are bonded together with mortar to form a wall.

Master Suite now Primary Suite

To be considered a primary suite, the room must have enough space for a sitting area, an in-room office, and an en-suite bathroom. The term commonly refers to a primary bedroom with a private bath attached.

MDF

Medium-density fiberboard is a wood material composed of hard and softwood residuals that can be denser than plywood but not as strong. It is commonly used for baseboards and other interior trims.

Membrane

A layer of material that is impermeable to water. Typically used on flat roofs. It can be made of synthetic rubber or PVC.

Mid-century Modern

A design popularized between 1930 and 1960 involves sleek lines and a futuristic yet organic style.

Millwork

Any wood product that was produced in a mill. For example, molding, doors, and trim.

Mini Split

An energy-efficient heating and cooling system has two components: an indoor fan coil and an outdoor compressor.

Miter Joint

It is a miter joint when two pieces of material are cut and joined at a 45-degree angle to form a 90-degree corner.

Molding

Decorative trim is used to frame or shape something.

Mortar

A stone binding paste is commonly used to join brick, concrete blocks, and decorative stones.

Mud Room

An entryway is found at the front or back door, often with a coat closet and easy-to-clean flooring, like linoleum.

N

Natural Gas

A gas mixture containing mostly methane. It is used to heat some homes and provides flame to gas-powered ovens and stovetops.

Net-Zero-Energy

Homes that produce as much renewable energy as they use over the course of a year. Energy comes from solar panels, and the home's energy needs are reduced with super-insulated walls and windows.

Nonbearing Wall

A wall that does not offer any structural support to the building.

O

On-Demand Hot Water Heater

An energy-efficient tankless water heater.

OSB

Oriented strand board is a wood product engineered by compressing wood strands and adhesives.

P

P-Trap

The curved portion of a drainpipe forms a water seal to block sewage gases from entering the home.

Paint

A permanent decorative liquid wall coating. It can be oil or latex based.

Particle Board

A more affordable substitute for plywood. Engineered from sawdust and resin.

Partition

A wall that divides a room into multiple parts.

Paver

Pieces of masonry are laid flat to make a pathway.

Pedestal Sink

A sink basin supported by a column.

Percolation Test

A test was performed by a soil engineer to determine if the ground could absorb liquid from a septic system.

Perimeter Drain

The perimeter drain is a drainage system installed in the ground surrounding the foundation of your home. The perimeter drain is usually connected to a sump pump that pumps out excess water.

Permeable Pavement

Paving material that allows stormwater to pass through. Often done with porous concrete or separated paving stone.

Permit

A city-issued document allowing a specific project to be done.

PEX

A plastic tubing system is used to supply pipes with water. Made of cross-linked polyethylene, PEX is flexible and heat resistant.

Pitch

The measurement of the steepness of a roof slope. It tells you how many inches the roof rises for every 12" of roof depth. A 12/12 roof would be very steep, while a 6/12 roof would be much less steep.

Plan View

In architectural plans, it is a view from the top, looking down.

Plans

In architecture and design, plans include drawings of the proposed building, specifications, and more. It is a complete set of guidelines needed to complete construction.

Plumb

A line that is perfectly vertical.

Plumber

A person hired to install or repair sewage or drainage piping and potable water.

Plumbing Rough

After the rough heat is installed, the plumbing contractor installs all plastic ABS drain and copper water lines, waste lines, shower pans, bathtubs, and gas piping to furnaces and fireplaces.

Plumbing Stack

A main plumbing pipe that runs vertically through multiple levels of flooring. Horizontal pipes on every floor connect to it. It can be a vent pipe to the roof or a drainage pipe that carries sewage down.

Plumbing Trim

The process of installing seals and fixtures occurs after the interior wall is finished being installed over the rough plumbing.

Plywood

A wooden panel made of multiple layers of veneer pressed together with adhesive.

Pocket Door

A sliding door that, when completely open, is hidden in the wall.

Porcelain Tile

A dense, less-porous clay formed and colored into flat sheets, it is often used for countertops and other bathroom surfaces.

Portland Cement

Cement is created by heating crushed limestone and clay into a solid brick and then grinding the brick into a powder. It is the main binder in many concretes and mortar mixtures.

Post and Beam

A support structure made of a few columns rather than that of stud framing support.

Post and Pier Foundation

The foundation system has short wooden support beams rather than concrete footers.

Primer

Primer is the first layer of paint applied when multiple layers are added. It helps hide small imperfections in the surface and provides a layer to which the finish paint can bind.

Punch List

A list of errors or oversights that a contractor should correct.

PVC

Plastic piping is made of Poly Vinyl Chloride.

Q

Quartz

A natural mineral made of silicon and oxygen. In interior design and construction, it usually refers to an engineered countertop surface made of crushed quartz and a small amount of hard-wearing resin and very resistant to staining.

Quartzite

An extremely hard natural metamorphic rock that contains quartz. It can be mined and milled into stone slabs for countertops.

R

R-Value

A measurement of how well a wall, layer of insulation, or other surfaces can resist a conductive heat flow. Often, the R-value of an entire wall assembly can be calculated.

Radiant Heating

Heat is transmitted by electromagnetic waves rather than conduction or convection. It is a gentle, even form of heat that most people find very comfortable. Radiant heat systems are commonly installed underneath flooring, either with an electric mat or hot-water tubing. Radiant heat panels can also be installed on a ceiling for an instant feeling of warmth. Radiant heat can save energy because it doesn't require the air in a room to be as warm for an occupant to feel warm.

Radon

A dense radioactive gas that naturally occurs in many parts of the world. A common source of lung cancer. Homes in radon-prone areas need to be assessed for radon, and steps must be made to ventilate the radon out of the home.

Rafter

Two-by-ten or 2x12 studs installed horizontally to support the roof load.

Rebar

Textured steel bars are set in concrete to support to concrete structures like foundations, footers, and walls.

Reclaimed Materials

Materials from a previous building are reused for a new project.

Recycled Materials

Materials from products that have reached the end of their useful life have been reprocessed to make a newer product.

Reinforced Concrete

Concrete that has been set with steel mesh or rebar to enforce strength.

Remediation

The act of stopping or reversing environmental damage such as mold or asbestos.

Retaining Wall

A structure built to retain soil. Commonly installed on properties that are on a slope.

Rim Joist

In relation to the framing system of a deck or flooring, a rim joist is Installed perpendicular to the joist and offers lateral support.

Risers

The vertical boards are placed to fill the space between stair treads.

Rough Carpentry

Base work done for a building like framing. As opposed to finish carpentry, which is the installation of trim and other items once the main structural work is done.

Rough-In

Plumbing, duct, or electrical work is set in place but not yet installed.

Rough Opening

The opening is made for a doorway or window before installing shims, drywall, trim, or siding.

S

Sanitary Sewer

A sewer system that collects sewage from the interior pipes. Not meant to hold storm drainage.

Schluter

A name-brand tile edge protector with a symmetrically rounded corner profile.

Scribing

The act of fitting and cutting woodwork to go on an irregular surface.

Second-Story Addition

Removing the roof and adding another level to a single-story home.

Section drawings

When looking at building plans, a section drawing shows a vertical slice of the home, including ceiling heights.

Semi-Gloss Paint

Paint that, when dry, has a moderate amount of shine. Semi-gloss paint is often applied to bathrooms and kitchens because it is easy to wipe down.

Septic System

An underground wastewater treatment tank. Built on site and size depending on the number of bedrooms in the home. The septic system promotes the organic breakdown of solid waste through an anaerobic process.

Setbacks

The minimum distance a building is to be placed from a street, alleyway, or sidewalk. This is partially a safety measure to protect the building.

Sewer Stub

The connecting point between your home's sewer line and the city's main sewer line.

Shake

A wooden shingle is created by splitting wood at the grain line. It is most commonly made with cedar or redwood.

Shaker Style

A traditional furniture style with tapered legs and clean lines, Shaker-style kitchen cabinet doors and drawer faces featuring a flat center panel and square edges have become very popular. Although it is a traditional style, it has also enjoyed contemporary popularity.

Sheathing

The installation of wood paneling on the exterior of the building's framing structure. This is usually done with plywood or OSB.

Sheen

A level of gloss or luster a surface has after the paint has dried.

Sheet Metal Ductwork

Metal ducts, round or square push hot or cold air from the furnace through the rest of the house.

Sheet Rock

A brand name of drywall paneling that encases the interior of the building. The drywall is made of calcium sulfate dihydrate and is layered front and back with thick sheets of paper.

Shim

A piece of scrap wood or metal wedged into a tight spot pushes a beam or frame into place.

Shingles

Roof coverings are made of asphalt, wood, slate, or tile, cut to size and layered in a way that protects the roof from natural elements.

Shower Pan

A waterproof barrier is installed under the shower basin to prevent leakage.

Side Sewer

The portion of the sanitary sewer line that runs from the house to the public sewer line is buried several feet underground and maintained by the homeowner.

Siding

Protective material installed on the exterior of the house. Also known as wall cladding.

Sill

The wood plate framing that lays flat against the foundation wall is installed with anchor bolts. This is usually done with treated lumber.

Single-Hung Window

A window with one opening pane or vent.

Skirting

Installing a wooden board along the base of an interior wall.

Skylight

Skylights are lighting and sometimes ventilation structures installed on the roof. Occasionally referred to as ceiling windows they come in many shapes and sizes for all types of roof shapes.

Slab

Another term for a paved concrete surface. For example, a driveway, garage floor, or basement floor.

Smart Home

A home that has a built-in automation system that controls the lighting, temperature, electronics, appliances, and security systems.

Soaking Tub

A soaking tub is a freestanding tub deep enough for you to be completely submerged. This is preferable to bathing in a standard tub, where your shoulders and knees are exposed.

Soffit

The material that lines the underside of the roof structure on an overhang extends past the exterior wall.

Soft Goods

Textiles with a soft texture, like carpet, linens, or curtains.

Softwood

Wood sourced from gymnosperm trees, such as conifers.

Soil Stack

The vertical plumbing carries sewage away from toilets and down to the drain. It is normally also extended up to the roof to vent.

Solid-Surface Countertops

A countertop made of marble dust and plastic resin. This creates a pore-less surface.

Sound Attenuation

The act of soundproofing a wall or floor with insulation and other products.

Space Planning

A part of the design process determining where furniture and appliances should be placed to work effectively with each other.

Specs

Specific information about your project, including signed agreements, design drafts, lists of subcontractors, and other details needed for the remodeling project.

Spray Foam Insulation

A chemical foam that can be sprayed directed onto the framing of a home. Spray foam is made of isocyanate and polyol resin, two chemicals that, when added together, expand and solidify 30 to 60 times the volume of the original liquid.

Square Footage

The area within the original floorplan is calculated by multiplying the width in feet by the length in feet.

Standing-Seam Metal Roof

Roofing is in the form of large metal sheets with raised vertical ribs that are set about one foot apart from each other. An extremely durable roofing material.

STFI

Standard fire and allied perils insurance. This type of home insurance covers fire, lightning, aircraft damage, explosion, sprinkler leakage, and many other adverse events.

Storm Window

A temporary or permanent second window layer that is installed on the exterior of the original window to offer protection from the elements.

Strike

The metal plate into which the bolt of a door's latch is slid. The strike is mounted on the door frame.

Structural Engineer

Engineers who are trained and licensed to design the framing and support of a building. A Structural Engineer is usually enlisted if a home requires major structural modifications.

Stucco

A plaster coating is used on the exterior of buildings.

Stud

A two-by-four or 2x6 is installed vertically on the framing system. It is also known as a wall stud and is attached to both the top and bottom horizontal support plates.

Sump Pump

A pump removes water accumulated in a sump or shallow depression. Sump pumps are common in basements that are prone to water intrusion.

Superintendent

The person leading a remodel or building project who works on site.

Supply Lines

The part of the piping or electrical system that runs from the city's supply to your home.

Switch Plate

The plastic (or metal) plate that covers interior wiring but allows a switch's toggle to protrude.

T

Taping

The act of sealing the cracks between drywall sheets. This is done with paper tape and joint compound.

Teardown

A teardown is the act of demolishing a home and clearing the lot to start new. It is sometimes necessary when there is extensive damage or rot or if the value of the lot is far greater than the home that currently sits upon it. In real estate, a teardown can also refer to a home in bad shape that will most likely be demolished by a new owner.

Tempered Glass

Strengthened glass that has undergone intense heating followed by a rapid cool down forces the glass into compression. Tempered glass is about four times stronger than standard glass and "pelletized" rather than shatters.

Termites

A colony of ant-like bugs that tunnel through wood. Termite infestations can quickly cause serious structural damage to a home.

Terrazzo

A flooring mixture of quartz, marble, granite, or glass chips. Terrazzo is bound with resin and then polished to a smooth surface. It is either poured in place or precast to fit a specific spot.

Thermostat

A thermostat is a device that detects and controls the temperature of an area. It can be manually or automatically adjusted.

Time-and-Materials Contract

A type of construction contract with no fixed price for the job. The final price will be calculated (usually at each billing cycle) based on the number of hours the contractor put in, the cost of materials, and the cost of subcontractors. The risk of cost overruns is placed on the homeowner.

Toe Nailing

Driving a nail in at an angle to hold floor joists to the plate.

Top Plate

A horizontal piece of the frame wall located at the top of the wall, the top plate supports rafters, ceiling joists, or other members of the frame.

Townhouse

A multi-level home on a small footprint that adjoins the adjacent home or homes.

Trade Only

Also "to the trade." Refers to dealers that sell furniture, fabrics, and other furnishings to designers only. Items are typically sold at a discount, and the designer marks them up in contrast with retail stores.

Trap

A plumbing fitting that is responsible for holding water to prevent air, gas, and vermin from backing up into the home through a fixture.

Trim

Finishing touches that mechanical contractors apply to complete their work including moldings, installation of interior doors, guard rails, shelves etc.

Truss

A premade assembly of beams and other elements that make up a part of a building. The most common is a roof truss.

Two-Story Addition

An addition to the side of a home. Often, the bottom floor of the addition will be an additional living space, while the top floor is an extra bedroom or master suite.

Trades

An umbrella term for skilled tradespeople, many of whom are licensed, such as electricians and plumbers. Other skilled trades, such as demolition, concrete work, and roofing, may or may not require professional licensing.

Treads

The top surface piece of a stair step.

U

U-Value

The measurement of the amount of heat lost, usually through a window. The lower the U-value, the more energy-efficient the window.

Underlayment

A material placed under flooring and roofing that protects the sub-layer from water damage and provides a smooth, even surface.

Universal Design

A design that makes the property and building accessible to all. Including the elderly, children and the disabled.

Urethane Paint

A paint coating whose properties are more elastic than that of a polyurethane which has a harder structure. The elastic properties of urethane paint help provide a glossy finish.

V

Vanity

Bathroom cabinetry that holds the sink and fixture while providing excess storage space.

Veneer

A very thin sheet of wood. Veneer is used in woodworking to make doors, flooring, and other finishes.

Vinyl Windows

PVC windows. Originating in the 1970's, vinyl windows are more affordable and require less maintenance than wood windows.

VR

A virtual reality hologram is used to portray remodel designs.

W

Walk-In Closet

A closet extending farther than that of a standard closet, allowing a person to enter. Walk-in closets are generally large enough for two people to share.

Walk-In Shower

This is a shower without an attached bathing tub. You can walk directly into it because it is level with the floor.

Walk-Through

The final inspection is to check for design or construction errors that may need fixing before the project is deemed to be complete.

Wall-Hung Toilet

A toilet was installed, with the tank hidden behind the interior wall. Wall-hung toilets are considered a modern and minimalist design.

Wallpaper

A decorative sheet of paper that is applied to an interior wall in many different ways. Some wallpaper has adhesive backing, while others require glue.

Warranty

A contract that covers an appliance or labor done to a home that offers protection from an assembly flaw. Most warranties offer free replacement and labor within a specified time limit.

Waste Pipe

The pipe carries waste from the home to the city's sewage system.

Water-Based Paint

Pigment and binder dissolved in water to be applied to interior walls.

Water Closet

A small room that has only a toilet. Water closets are often attached to master baths.

Water Main

The pipe that delivers water from the city supplies pipe to the home.

Waterproofing

Adding barrier material or sealant protects the exterior of your foundation from water damage caused by direct contact with soil. This involves excavating around the foundation all the way down to the bottom, applying a sealant, and routing the excess water through a drainage system.

WC

An abbreviation for water closet. (See water closet.)

Weatherization

The act of improving the exterior of your home to offer better insulation to keep energy consumption low. This involves caulking, adding new insulation, storm windows and doors, and adding weather stripping.

Weatherstrip

Thin plates of metal or other material surround doors and windows to keep excess air from flowing in and out of the home.

Weep Holes

Small holes that allow moisture to escape.

Wet Bathroom

A bathroom that has a shower without water barrier walls or floor lips. The walls and floor of a wet bath are usually tiled.

Whitewood

A term that is used by cabinet makers for secondary utility lumber. It is used for unseen things like toe kick framing, cleats, webbing, and brackets. There are several different tree species that are considered whitewood, such as pine, poplar, and spruce. When whitewood is used for framing, it should be stamped "SPF."

Whole-House Fan

A ventilation system that involves a vent and tube that takes cool air from throughout the house and pushes it into the attic to support the even distribution of cool air throughout the home.

Whole-House Remodel

Renovation of an entire home, all the way down to the studs. This is commonly done on outdated homes with strong framing structures.

Woodwork

The wooden parts of a home, including framing, trim, doors, etc.

Z

Zone

Some HVAC systems have zones, which are areas of the home that are independently temperature controlled.

Zoning

A government-issued property label that limits the use of said property. Examples include single-family use, residential, high-rise, etc.

About the Author

With 29 years and counting, Danette Galvis has built her Real Estate career with experience and knowledge in multiple areas of the industry!

She brings expertise in property management, relocation services, custom home building, real estate print advertising, home design, home sales, general contracting, and real estate investing!

In recent years, she has focused on being a fearless "Mrs. Fix-it" as general contractor on her active deals, as a Real Estate Agent with eXp Realty, and as the Flipping & remodel Coach for the Women's Real Estate Investing Network.

Her *not-so-secret*, secret is her struggle with addiction! Being sober for almost a decade, Danette has been able to keep her health in sobriety, at the forefront of it all!

After being in an in-patient Medial treatment facility and then a Sober Living home, it has become her mission to serve others in sobriety and help them find financial freedom in real estate investing.

By writing this book, Danette is leaving a legacy for her family, and she prays it will bring others to freedom and glory to God!

Danette lives in Dallas, Texas, with her family, where she does most of her investing. She plans to open Sober Living homes in the Dallas area!

Please contact her if you want to purchase quantities of Kingdom RehabHER, interview her, or book Danette to speak at your event.

Connect with Danette

www.kingdomrehabher.com

info@kingdomrehabher.com

@DanetteGalvis

@DanetteBundschuGalvis

Danette Bundschu Galvis

www.ingramcontent.com/pod-product-compliance
Lightning Source LLC
Chambersburg PA
CBHW062218080426
42734CB00010B/1931